Silhouette of Dion Boucicault
at the age of five

The Career of
Dion Boucicault

By
Townsend Walsh

Benjamin Blom
New York

DUNLAP SOCIETY PUBLICATIONS

First published New York 1915
By the Dunlap Society
Reissued 1967 by
Benjamin Blom, Inc. New York 10452
Library of Congress Catalog Card #67-28848

PRINTED IN THE U.S.A.

Contents

Contents

Contents

[ix]

Contents

Contents

[xi]

Contents

List of Illustrations

—

The Society is indebted to Mr. Evert Jansen Wendell for the
loan of the photographs from which the illustrations
in this book have been made—from his well-
known dramatic collection.

[xiii]

Preface

DION BOUCICAULT!

The name itself is an ear-filler, a patronymic devised to invest the wearer with the subtle, magical qualities of a necromancer.

When Boucicault wrote a letter to Disraeli demanding in the name of the Irish nation and the author of "The Shaughraun" the immediate release of the Fenian prisoners, then under sentence for treason, the British Prime Minister ignored the modest missive. But some days after, at a reception when the name of Boucicault chanced to be mentioned, Disraeli turned round to his secretary and inquired: "Boucicault! Boucicault! Where have I heard that name before? Is it some one in the conjuring business?"

A conjurer he was in the best sense of the term; a mighty magician; a wizard of wondrous skill.

For a period of fifty years Dion Boucicault stood prominent in the world of the stage. He fed half the theatres of London and New York with the products of his pen. He utilized everything he read in novels, and adapted everything he saw in the Paris theatres. His enormous capacity for work equalled his superabundant activity. His gift of discerning what the public wanted was matched by his inexhaustible facility in supplying that want.

A man dowered to a high degree with all the attributes that go to make a masterful playwright!

Boucicault's talent was a marketable commodity. His earliest work proved his inborn theatrical instinct and brought him revenue and glory. Before he was twenty he had caught the trick of playwriting with facile elegance, and his dramatic labor for half a century covers every species of stage literature.

"How often," remarks Mr. William Archer, "have playgoers of the younger generation been surprised to learn that such and such a play, which to them seemed the relic of bygone ages, was the work of Boucicault!"

Yet measuring the longevity of his best work by that of his contemporaries, "London Assurance" and "Old Heads and Young Hearts" have outlived four-fifths of the plays of their day; while the Irish dramas are entwined to the temple of the legitimate with the tenacity of ivy on a round-tower.

A few years ago Mr. George Bernard Shaw delivered a lecture in London on "The Stage Irishman." He had a tolerant good word for Boucicault's Irishman, and condescendingly promised to give us, some day or another, the genuine article. In the course of time he gave us "John Bull's Other Island"; and Mr. Arnold Daly, who produced it in New York, spent a pretty penny in mounting it lavishly and tastefully. The few people who went to see it either fell fast asleep early in the evening or stayed awake to be wearied to boredom. Mr. Shaw's Stage Irishman proved a didactic bore, and didactic bores are the fell fates of the stage. Boucicault was vindicated.

Posterity seems to have practically decided that his Irish plays are the achievements upon which Boucicault's fame will ultimately rest. One of the most remarkable personalities in the history of the theatre, he was one of the most versatile; his range was of the widest, and he succeeded in every department of the realm of the stage; but it was as an actor of Irish parts and as a writer of Irish plays that he gained a place in the dramatic hierarchy.

With the shamrock for its symbol, Boucicault's fame rests secure, and Ireland may claim him as her peculiarly national property.

It would require a series of volumes of the scope of the present book to tell of his life work in an exhaustive way. My aim and purpose has been to give as much authentic information as could be condensed into an unreasonably small space. Every actor I have met in the last twenty years, who ever played with Boucicault, I have pumped dry. Everything in print about Boucicault that I could lay hold of has been noted and weighed for its worth. I am greatly indebted to Mr. William J. Lawrence, who has rendered invaluable service in delving into the archives of the Dublin Record Office in quest of statistics that might shed some light on Boucicault's parentage.

Mystery shrouds Boucicault's birth and ancestry, and scandal steps in with the ready explanation that he was born out of wedlock. To some persons scandal is unctuously nourishing, but I am not one of these; and it is in no ready spirit that I set forth the facts that tend to prove Boucicault to have been the natural son of Dr. Dionysius Lardner.

Days devoted to careful research in Dublin have failed to establish positively the date of Dion's birth. Nothing appertaining to his birth can be found in documentary evidence. However, the Record Office in the Four Courts, Dublin, shed some light on his antecedents. The negative evidence of the census returns and the old Dublin Directories and the authentic data of Mr. Arthur Darley have enabled me to speak with conviction about his parentage.

My biographical duty would be only partially fulfilled if I neglected to tell in plain terms the very strong reasons for believing Boucicault to have been born out of wedlock. But I have extenuated nothing nor set down aught in malice, and in that reflection I find a warrant for complete candor in discussing this matter.

Dion Boucicault in His Study

The Career of
Dion Boucicault

The Career of Dion Boucicault

CHAPTER I

Origin of the Boursiquots or Bourcicaults—The family
in Dublin—Mystery of Dion's parentage—Was he
born in 1820 or 1822?—Strong evidence to prove
that he was a love-child—His reputed father—The
Darley family—Dr. Dionysius Lardner.

"ARE you an Irishman?" somebody once asked
Dion Boucicault; to which Boucicault replied
with much majesty of manner, "Sir, nature did me
that honor."

That Boucicault was an Irishman indeed, and a
sincere patriot into the bargain, none would dare
dispute. His name, to be sure, is French; but what
of that, since his nature was thoroughly Hibernian? A bear may be christened "Teddy" without
ceasing to be a bear; and there is this fine power
in the quality of the Celt, that no lapse of time or
change of climate can tame the true Irish out of
him. Marshal MacMahon belongs to Limerick
still, though his forefathers drank the breath of
Burgundy for over two hundred years. The Irish
who fought in the armies of France, Spain and
Austria never lost their Celtic traits. One whiff

of the bog expels all alien races. And Dion Boucicault, despite his French name and ancestry, was
as true a son of the land that gave him birth as if
no mail-clad Boucicault had ever borne the baton
of Guienne into the fray of Agincourt.

So it is with the Boucicaults in Ireland and not
in France that we must concern ourselves. Emi-
grating from Tours in the south of France on the
revocation of the Edict of Nantes, they forthwith
settled in Ireland. I have traced one of Dion's
ancestors through the old Dublin newspapers, a
haberdasher who kept a shop at No. 1 Essex
Bridge for over thirty years. Here is his advertisement from "Faulkner's Dublin Journal," 1764:

"James Boursiquot, Haberdasher, begs leave to
acquaint the Public that he has removed from the
Upper Blind Quay to the New House at the Foot
of Essex Bridge, next door to Mr. Furnace,
Woollen Draper, & that he will use all the Means in
his Power to merit a continuation of their Favour.
*N. B. Very good unfurnished Lodgings to be let
in said house.*"

This advertisement was frequently repeated during that year. The same advertisement shows that
he was still at Essex Bridge in May, 1772. He
was doubtless the James Boursiquot who adver-
tised in a similar way in "Faulkner's Journal" of
February 28, 1799, where he further adds that he
has served the Dublin public for many years.

Dion is generally said to have been born at 47
Lower Gardiner Street in 1822. The "Dictionary
of National Biography" suggests two dates for the

event—December 26, 1820, and December 20,
1822, but fails to proffer any evidence. Now, as
will be shown subsequently, the earlier date is far
more likely the correct one. It is as absurd to put
trust in the fiction that he was nineteen years old
when he wrote "London Assurance" as it is to
believe that this was his first play. The conclusive
evidence of persons who knew of him in the provinces before he came to London proves that he
dabbled in play-writing and wrote several plays
which were acted and in which he himself appeared in Bristol, Hull, Brighton and other provincial towns.

An anonymous contributor to the "London
Evening Herald" of September 2, 1905, writing
on "The Mystery of Dion Boucicault," says: "Mysterious, indeed, are his family antecedents. In
America at the time of his death it was openly
stated that the brilliant dramatist was a love-child.
Gossips did not hesitate to aver that Dr. Dionysius
Lardner of encyclopedic fame, after whom the child
was called, who made himself his nominal guar-
dian and was responsible for his education, stood
in nearer relation to the boy than he cared to avow.
In character and idiosyncracies there were certainly many points of resemblance between the
pundit and the playwright. Although satirized by
Thackeray as a literary empiric, Lardner did the
state service as a popularizer of science, doing
much the kind of work in his own day that Grant
Allen has done in ours. The average scientist is
not endowed with the proclivities of Don Juan,

but it must be confessed that Lardner was not of the monogamic way of thinking. In 1820 he separated by mutual consent from his first wife, *née* Cecelia Flood. The date of the separation synchronizes curiously with one of the conjectured dates of Dion Boucicault's birth. Many years later Dr. Lardner eloped with a military officer's wife, a Mrs. Heaviside, with whom he had long been carrying on an intrigue. Subsequently, in 1849, after he had been mulcted in heavy damages, he married the lady. These facts go to reveal certain weaknesses in Lardner's character, and tend to show the probability of his being involved in a *liaison* at the period of Boucicault's birth." The writer then goes on to argue that if Dion was a natural son, Boursiquot might have been his mother's name.

In 1818–1819 there was a firm of wholesale wine merchants called Boursiquot & Woodruffe at 10 Jervis Street. From an entry in Wilson's Dublin Directory, issued annually at this time, we learn that Samuel Smith Boursiquot was the name of Woodruffe's partner.

He it was who was the reputed author of Dion's being. According to the printed Marriage List in the Dublin Record Office, Samuel Smith Boursiquot in 1813 married Anne Maria Darley. She belonged to a family of *literati*, and was the sister of the Reverend Charles Darley and George Darley, the poet. Their father was Arthur Darley of the Scalp, County Wicklow. The family is believed to have come into Ireland with the Ulster plantation.

Carlyle had a high opinion of George Darley,[1] the poet, and said that he was little inferior to Tennyson. This point is important in showing that there were literary gifts on Dion's mother's side, but none on the Boursiquots' side. In fact, the Boursiquots seem to have been mediocrities.

Mr. Arthur Darley, a well-known Irish musician of the present day, living at Rathgar, Dublin, and a collateral descendant of Dion, has graciously furnished me with some exclusive details concerning the family. According to him, Samuel Smith Boursiquot separated from his wife in 1819.[2] Shortly afterward he failed in his business and obtained a situation as gauger in the Excise. This sounds plausible, as a wholesale wine merchant would have received a proper training for that

---

[1] George Darley was born in Dublin in 1795. He entered Trinity College in 1815 and graduated in 1820. In 1822 he settled in London, and in the same year produced his "Errours of Ecstacie." Then followed "The Labours of Idleness" (prose and verse) in 1826; "Sylvia," a fairy drama, in 1827; "Nepenthe," an indescribable rhapsody, in 1839; "Thomas à Becket" in 1840 and "Ethelstan" in 1841, both tragedies. He died in London, 1846. Says T. W. Rolleston in "A Treasury of Irish Poetry": "George Darley's work won cordial recognition from his brother poets of the day. Tennyson offered to pay the expenses of publishing his verse; Browning was inspired by 'Sylvia'; and Carey, the translator of Dante, thought that drama the finest poem of the day."

[2] If they separated in 1819, Dion could not have been born in 1822 and have been a legitimate son. This same year—1819—Dionysius Lardner went to lodge with her, having parted from his wife.

work. As gauger he went to Athlone, where he committed suicide by throwing himself out of the window of the hotel where he lived. There is also a legend of his being taken *flagrante delicto* and, escaping from an enraged husband, of meeting his death by jumping from the window of the bed-chamber.

Now remark that late in 1820, at the period when the Boursiquots had separated, Dr. Dionysius Lardner was living in Lower Gardiner Street, the reputed birth street of Dion. But if the dramatist was born there, it must have been before May, 1821, for the census was taken at that period, and in the return No. 47 is marked as "Uninhabited—To be let." Lower Gardiner Street is in the parish of St. Thomas. I looked up the baptismal registers of that parish from 1819 to 1823, but found no trace of any child called Boursiquot, Boucicault or Lardner. If illegitimate, Dion may never have been baptized.

And now a word about the worthy Lardner.[1] He was born in 1793, and his first wife, Cecelia Flood, was the granddaughter of the Right Honorable Henry Flood. They had three children. I find by the Dublin Directories that "D. Lardner" was living in 1818 at 12 Russell Street. Later he took holy orders, and in the Directory for 1821 (details for which were collected late in 1820) the

---

[1] Described by Thackeray as "spending all his money on clothes and in giving treats to the ladies, of whom he was outrageously fond." *Vide* "The History of Dionysius Diddler," by Thackeray; first published in 1864 in the "Autographic Mirror."

address of "the Rev. D. Lardner" is given as 47
Lower Gardiner Street and 29 Trinity College.
From that date till 1833 his address is given as
Trinity College only.

The "Dictionary of National Biography" says
that in 1820 Dr. Lardner had separated from his
wife, who did not, however, get a divorce till
twenty years after, when he carried on an intrigue
with a cavalry officer's wife and finally eloped
with her. The husband brought an action for criminal conduct and recovered eight thousand pounds
damages; he also got a bill of divorce from Parlia-
ment. Lardner then married Mrs. Heaviside, by
whom he had two daughters. About 1849 he went
to America on a lecture tour, which proved a financial success. The "Dictionary of National Biography" thus sums up Lardner: "Not an original or
profound thinker, but a man of great and versatile
activity."

This succinct commentary, by the way, applies
with equal pertinence to Dion Boucicault.

Now for some evidence showing the likelihood
of Lardner's responsibility for Dion's existence.
Lardner not only supervised the boy's education
and paid the cost of his schooling, but subsequently
articled him to his business as a civil engineer.
We can scarcely believe that he was actuated by
pure philanthropy or by a generous interest in the
future of a precocious child. Lardner was by no
means well-to-do, and had already a wife and
three children to support. It seems more likely
that Lardner brought up Dion because he was his

own,[1] and because Mrs. Samuel Smith Boursiquot had no claim for him on her husband.

Dion (on the authority of persons who remember the family) had no physical, intellectual or moral resemblance to his uterine brothers. They were big, lumbering men. William Boursiquot was of a religious turn and disliked the theatre. He was found dead of heart disease at Waterloo Station in an incoming railway train. Two other sons, twins, Arthur and George, were sent out to Australia, where they went on the press. George founded and edited the leading morning journal in Melbourne, while Arthur founded the "Northern Argus" of Queensland.

That Anne Darley was the dramatist's mother there can be no doubt. But of the two possible fathers—Samuel Smith Boursiquot and Dionysius Lardner—all facts point to the latter.

And now, before closing a disagreeable and by no means interesting, but altogether necessary chapter in our author's life, let us confront two potent facts and then draw our own conclusions. If Dion was the lawful offspring of Samuel Smith Boursiquot, who separated from Mrs. Boursiquot in 1819, he could never have come into the world as late as 1822. If, on the other hand, he was born in that year, and in the house generally recorded by biographers, he was undoubtedly the natural son of Dionysius Lardner.

[1] Mr. D. J. O'Donoghue of Dublin, publisher and author, tells me that Dion's first contributions to literature appeared in the "London University Magazine" and were signed Dionysius Lardner Boursiquot."

CHAPTER II

*School-days — Pranks with Charles Lamb Kenney —
"Napoleon's Old Guard" acted at Brentford by his
school-fellows — Extraordinary precocity — Becomes an
actor in 1839 — Barton Hill's reminiscences of Boucicault at the Cheltenham and Gloucester Theatres —
Rôles enacted at Hull — An adaptation of "Jack Sheppard" — Plays Jack himself under the nom de théâtre
of "Lee Moreton."*

WITH this introduction, we allow Boucicault
to tell in his own words his life up to 1883,
as chronicled in the "New York World" of Sun-
day, May 15, 1887:

"The life of a man does not begin at the moment
of his birth. For a few years he is a vegetable.
Then he becomes an animal, and at last—as the
grub turns into the fly—his mind unfolds its wings
and he lives under the sun.

"My first experience of life was at a school at
Hampstead in 1833, then a rural village three
miles from London, now swallowed into the me-
tropolis. It was a private school kept by Mr.
Hessey, the father of the master of Merchant
Tailors' School, and a dignitary of the church.

"There were seven or eight of us. I was the
stupidest and worst of the lot. In vain the patient,
gentle old man tried to find some way into my
mind; it was a hopeless task. It was not there.

It was wandering into day-dreams and was not to be confined in a bare room, a pile of grammars and slates. Oh, how I hated Latin! The multiplication table was a bed of torture! Oh, for the sunny solitude of a dry ditch and a volume of the 'Seven Champions of Christendom'! I wonder if that wonderful book exists still and is read by boys of ten—if there are any boys of ten.

"At fourteen I was removed from Hessey's to the London University, but boarded in Euston Square, near the school, with the Rev. Henry Stebbing, a most amiable man and a historian of note. What a life I led him! There were two boys in this great school among the four or five hundred scholars that were distinguished for being exemplary vagabonds, worthless, idle rogues. One to whom courtesy obliges me to give precedence was Charles Lamb Kenney, the son of the dramatist, and I need not name the other. There was a black hole in this school for solitary confinement of incorrigible pupils. We disputed for that lodging. It was rarely empty. We employed our leisure in prison by covering the walls with lampoons on the professors. Those composed by myself were very libelous. I signed the worst specimens with Kenney's name. He did his best in the same line over my signature. We used to call it our mural literature. One day, however,—how pleasant it is to recall such boyish nonsense!—the Latin class was waiting for the arrival of our master, a fiery, vehement red-haired German named Rainbach. I crept up to the great blackboard on which the master used to write, in English, verse which we were called on to translate as an exercise into Latin metre, and wrote in bold chalk letters:

" 'Rainbach was fiery, hot,
    Irascible and proudish;
His mother was a mustard-pot,
    And his father a horseradish.'

" 'The gentlemen will please put that in iambics.'

"The roar of laughter elicited by the doggerel had not subsided when we heard the voice of the head-master, Mr. Key, accompanying Rainbach up the stair into the class-room. I had no time to efface the damning evidence, but regained my usual seat at the foot of the class—a place, by the way, constantly disputed by Kenney. We occupied it by turns. The two dons advanced amidst dead silence and faced the slate. It was an awful moment when Mr. Key turned to scan the class. His face was purple with the effort to suppress his laughter. But he mastered it. 'Young gentlemen,' he said, 'I desire that the writer of those lines shall stand out.' With one movement, Kenney and I stepped out together, while he assumed a look of penitence and guilt. 'What!' roared Key, 'both of you? That is impossible.' I insisted upon bearing the blame alone, and appealed to the class. The head-master said gravely that to hold up a professor to ridicule in this manner was a capital offence, and ordered my school-fellow to sit down. Kenney, with a face I shall never forget, lifted his eyes

to the skylight and declaimed in a voice imitating
precisely the well-known tones of Mr. Key himself:

> " 'Hos ego versiculos feci
> Tulit alter honorem,'

and putting on a dejected air, regained his seat.
The effect was irresistible. Rainbach joined in the
roar of laughter with all his big heart. I was con-
demned to rub out the lines, and I tendered a very
humble and sincere apology to one of the finest
scholars and best of men. Let those young men
who read these lines pardon the garrulity of old
age. When they are old they will value such
boyish memories, however trifling, as I do.

"So it was that in 1838 I found myself removed
to a collegiate school in Brentford, kept by a Dr.
Jamieson. In the summer of that year we had an
exhibition at which the boys played 'Pizarro.' The
part of *Rolla* fell to me, and then, for the first
time, my mind seemed to soar. I wanted to play
every part in the piece, but had to content myself
by teaching all the rest how their parts should be
given. I never controlled so obedient and enthusiastic a crowd. We wanted an after-piece. I
offered to write one, and I wrote the little sketch
(afterward played at the Princess's Theatre, London) called 'Napoleon's Old Guard.' The success
attending this exhibition settled my mind. I would
be an actor, and nothing else.

"On leaving Brentford, I was apprenticed to
Dr. Lardner as a civil engineer, and became his

pupil.[1]   Then I floated back to my early love, the
stage.   In 1839, breaking away from all trammels
and taking a few pounds pocket money, I started
for Cheltenham, Gloucester and Bristol, where I
found an engagement to act and appeared in a few
parts with encouraging success.   After a few
weeks I wandered away to Hull and to Brighton,
returning to London in the spring of 1840, penniless, and with a portmanteau chiefly filled with
hopes."

We must here interrupt Boucicault's reminiscences and let Mr. Barton Hill, admirable actor
and reliable stage historian, narrate the story of
Boucicault's professional début:

"My father having taken the management of the
Cheltenham and Gloucester theatres, Gloucester-
shire, England, it was here that I, as a child, first
met with a young man, then known as Lee Moreton, but afterward famous as the gifted author and
actor, Dion Boucicault, or, as he wrote his own
autograph in February, 1842, in a letter to my
father (which letter I possess), Bourcicault—
omitting the 'r' later in life.   From my parents
I learned how they came to hear of him in the
spring of 1837: This young man, Lee Moreton,
was constantly begging my father to give him
some part, however small, to appear in, and, if he
succeeded in it, an engagement to follow.   My

[1] At the London University, with which Dionysius Lard-
ner was connected.   According to family tradition, young
Boucicault helped to lay the first railway line between
Harrow and London.

father gave him the part of *Tressel* in 'Richard III'
(the part in which Edwin Booth made his first
appearance on any stage, at the Boston Museum,
September 10, 1849, to his father's *Richard III*).

"How far the young man succeeded as *Tressel,*
I do not know, but some weeks later a performance
was given—'Under the patronage of Lieutenant-
Colonel Pym' (I remember the bill announcing it
distinctly)—when Massinger's 'A New Way to
Pay Old Debts' was given, the part of *Sir Giles
Overreach* 'By a Young Gentleman of this City.'
The performance was quite a success, and it turned
out that *Sir Giles* was the *Tressel* of some weeks
before.   Mr. Lee Moreton was engaged at once,
and soon after became a protégé of my father's,
who thus came into correspondence for some few
years with this young man's guardians, legal ad-
visers of the celebrated scientist and writer, Dr.
Dionysius Lardner, who, as is known, eloped with
the wife of an English officer, afterward married
her, and in 1840 settled down in Paris.   At just
about this time Lee Moreton became known as
D. L. or Dionysius Lardner Boucicault, or Bourcicault.

"In the spring of 1837 my father leased the
Theatre Royal, Brighton, in Sussex, so we all
moved to that city in June, Mr. Lee Moreton trav-
eling with us, and stopped over in London to
witness the coronation of Queen Victoria in June
of that year.

"I remember well the magnificence of that pro-
cession, and also that, as Her Majesty came to

Dion Boucicault as *Michael O'Dowd* in "Daddy O'Dowd"

reside at the Royal Pavilion, Brighton, I had many opportunities of seeing her and riding over the Downs (at, of course, a respectful distance) after the young Queen before her marriage.

"Soon after the opening of the season, my father presented Mr. Lee Moreton to the public of Brighton as *Sir Giles Overreach* for a few nights, and then as *Rory O'More,* in Samuel Lover's dramatization of his own novel—his first appearance on the stage in an Irish character, in which line of parts he afterward became so world-famous. He did not play again at that time, but devoted himself earnestly to dramatic writing, and in due course of time handed my father the manuscript of his first effort.[1] My father was so well pleased with it that he offered to produce it if certain changes that he pointed out as essential should be made, but the young author, most fortunately as it happened, declined to make them, and my father then advised him to take the 'Royal Mail' at once for London (the London and Brighton Railroad was not completed till about a year later), and offer his piece to the managers

[1] Probably "A Lover by Proxy," which he afterward submitted to Charles Mathews. "We are gutted with farces," said the comedian. "What we want nowadays is a good five-act comedy. Now if I could find such a part as you have sketched here in a modern comedy, there would be room for such a work." A month later Boucicault returned with a big roll of manuscript under his coat-tail. "There is the five-act comedy you wanted," he said. "There is a part in it similar to that I wrote for you in 'A Lover by Proxy.'" *Harry Lawless* had been expanded to *Dazzle.*

of the best metropolitan theatres, to whom he
would give him letters of introduction. He did
so without loss of time. I remember well accompanying my father to see him off, happy
with youthful hope, his manuscript and letters
in the old-fashioned carpet-bag of those days,
that I was carrying for him. The guard tossed it
on the top of the 'Royal Blue' coach, and he clam-
bered to the box-seat beside George Gilbert, the
famous crack 'whip' of the London coach. How
well I recall my sorrow as I witnessed his departure! I was very fond of him; he had driven me
to school; he had taught me my first moves at
chess; had forgiven my too frequent confiscation
of his pet cigars, and had made me *particeps crimi-
nis* in his extravagance, that my dear mother would
constantly scold him for, but to no purpose, for
upon receipt from his guardians of his quarterly
allowance, he would bring home the choicest and
most expensive imported fruits, cakes and sweet-
meats. I say 'home,' for he lived with us at Rut-
land House, Marine Parade. Mother would scold
and scold, and at last refuse to touch them; so did
my sister, Rosalie, but I, having 'no compunctious
visitings of nature' to 'shake my fell purpose,'
would help him to fill us 'top full' of these luxuries.

"He was a handsome youth, and generous to a
fault.

"But to return to the three-act comedy: Boucicault—as he must henceforth be known—on reach-
ing London, wisely selected the Covent Garden
Theatre for his field of action, and through my

father's letter of introduction obtained an interview with Mr. Charles Mathews, the stage manager and the then recently married husband of Mme. Vestris, the lessee; he was at once promised an early perusal and careful consideration of his manuscript, and given the freedom of the theatre before and behind the curtain in the interim. The consequence of which followed as a matter of course: he immediately fell, a willing victim, at the feet of the celebrated Mrs. Nisbet, the adored of the London public, and, among the members of the company, to whom he was presented, found an instant friend and companion in John Brougham. Both of them Dublin-born, Boucicault some ten years the younger, they were kindred spirits and lodged in the same house.

"Mathews refused 'A Lover by Proxy,' but, a month later, when the persistent author presented himself at the stage door of Covent Garden Theatre with 'London Assurance,' he was cordially received. Mathews and his wife read the play and promptly accepted it.

"Soon afterward manager and author met to talk over the cast and arrange the first reading to the company, and, to his amazement, Boucicault found that his idol had not been given the part of *Grace*. Mr. Mathews explained that as there were only two female parts in the piece—*Grace Harkaway* and *Pert,* her maid—his wife, Mme. Vestris, must be the *Grace,* adding that he regretted that there had not been a third part written which he could give Mrs. Nisbet. Without a moment's hesitation, Dion obtained permission to withdraw his piece for a few days that he might think out what might perhaps be done, and hurried to his lodgings to work night and day until, in an incredibly short space of time, he returned with another manuscript, the part of *Lady Gay* to be given to Mrs. Nisbet, the character of *Dolly Spanker,* her husband, also added.   The delightful racy business which these changes brought about was perfectly arranged, and, as a crown, the title of the work was given as 'London Assurance.'   Thus to a boyish infatuation we owe the creation of *Lady Gay Spanker*.

"The 'Century Cyclopedia of Names' gives the date of Boucicault's birth as 'December 26, 1822'; if so, he was but a month or two over fourteen years old when he appeared as *Sir Giles Overreach,* which one may well misdoubt.   It also states that 'Mr. John Brougham claimed a share in the authorship of "London Assurance,"' but I had from Mr. Brougham's own lips (for I knew him intimately) that he claimed only the friendly suggestions of an expression or piece of comedy business here and there."

But in thus quoting Mr. Hill's comments on "London Assurance," I am forestalling events by at least a couple of years.   Other provincial engagements intervened, among them a lengthy stay at Hull, in proof of which I have in my possession a file of the Hull play-bills of the year 1839, in which the name of Lee Moreton frequently occurs.   Among the parts which he enacted while a member of the stock company at Hull were: *Tim Moore*, in the farce "The Irish Lion"; *Trip*, in "The School for Scandal"; *Osric*, in "Hamlet"; *Lamp*, in "Wild Oats"; *Gerald Pepper*, in "The White Horse of the Peppers"; *Terrence O'Connolly*, in "His First Champagne"; *Captain O'Cutter*, in Colman's comedy "The Jealous Wife"; and *Phelim* in the farce "23 St. John Street."

Most interesting of all was his appearance at Hull in the title rôle of a dramatization by himself of Ainsworth's "Jack Sheppard." This criminal romance, which made its author one of the literary lions of his day, first appeared serially in "Bentley's Miscellany," starting in 1839. Thackeray's indictment of "Jack Sheppard," which is contained in the article on Fielding that he contributed to the "Times," was more than usually savage and truculent: "Ainsworth dared not paint his hero as the scoundrel he knew him to be. He must keep his brutalities in the background, else the public morals would be outraged, and so he produced a book quite absurd and unreal, and infinitely more immoral than any Fielding ever wrote. 'Jack Sheppard' is immoral because it is decorous." This arraignment did not interfere in any way with the overwhelming popularity of the book. When we recall that the sales of "Jack Sheppard" exceeded those of "Oliver Twist," which appeared about the same time, and that Thackeray, conscious of his own great powers, was daily wincing under unappreciation and repulse, some of the irritability of the future author of "Vanity Fair" may be understood. The year 1839 saw many London theatres, where melodrama was the staple dish, doing a "Jack Sheppard" piece. At one and the same time seven different dramatic versions of Ainsworth's romance were being acted in London. Buckstone's dramatization, which is probably the best, was first produced at the Adelphi on October 28, 1839. This was a pronounced success, partly due to Mrs. Keeley's acting as *Jack,* and to the singing of Paul Bedford, who popularized Rodwell's "Jolly Nose."

When the play was at the height of its success, the Lord Chamberlain was induced to forbid its representation, and he formally notified all managers that for the future all plays on the subject were interdicted. This action of the censor has been ridiculed, and, indeed, to people of to-day it seems as if very little harm could result from the dramatic idealization of Ainsworth's housebreaker. But we must remember that plays of this sort stand on a dangerous border-line. They may be harmless or harmful, according to circumstances. In 1839 the whole condition of the lower classes was different from what it is at the present day. The antagonism between rich and poor was intense; the masses were grossly ignorant and shamefully neglected; and a false picture of life on the stage, like "Jack Sheppard," was acclaimed and applauded by hundreds as true and correct.

As in most of the "Jack Sheppard" plays, Boucicault—or Lee Moreton, as he then called himself —brought his curtain up on Cruikshank's picture of *Jack* carving his name on a cross-beam in Owen Wood's carpenter shop. The authentic play-bill, which I have in my possession, would seem to indicate that young Lee Moreton's version followed the main incidents of the story in much the same way as Buckstone's adaptation.

CHAPTER III

"London Assurance"—How it came to be written and acted—Its remarkable cast—Thackeray's parody of the play.

DURING his first year in London, the youth lived anyhow, drifting from one poor lodging to another, selling the little he had to obtain the means of life, but refusing to return to Dublin to his mother's home. During that winter he wrote the comedy "London Assurance."

It was a boyish performance, as he tells us, a flood of animal spirits. It was written in penny copy-books, sometimes in pencil when the ink froze and he had to creep into bed for warmth.

Charles Mathews was then in power at Covent Garden Theatre. He read "London Assurance," and accepted it at once. A few days after the comedy was called for reading in the greenroom. The cast included Farren, George Bartley, Anderson, Charles Mathews, Robert Keeley, Mme. Vestris and Mrs. Nisbet. They were all there; no such group of actors of comedy has perhaps since assembled together.

COMPLETE ORIGINAL CAST

Sir Harcourt Courtly . . .	WILLIAM FARREN.
Max Harkaway	GEORGE BARTLEY.
Charles Courtly	JAMES ANDERSON.
Dolly Spanker	ROBERT KEELEY.

Dazzle		CHARLES MATHEWS.
Mark Meddle		JOHN PRITT HARLEY.
Cool		MR. BRINDAL.
Simpson		R. W. HONNER.
Martin		MR. AYLIFFE.
Solomon Isaacs		ALFRED WIGAN.
Lady Gay Spanker		MRS. NISBET.
Grace Harkaway		MME. VESTRIS.
Pert		MRS. HUMBY.

The last important revival of "London Assurance" took place at St. James's Theatre, London, on the afternoon of Friday, July 27, 1913, when a picked cast of "stars" appeared on behalf of King George's Pension Fund for Actors and Actresses. The King and Queen were present. To old playgoers it will perhaps prove interesting to compare some of the names given above with those of the modern "stars." For them it is worth while to append the cast:

Sir Harcourt Courtly . . .		HERBERT TREE.
Charles Courtly		GODFREY TEARLE.
Dazzle		H. B. IRVING.
Dolly Spanker		JAMES WELCH.
Max Harkaway		HENRY AINLEY.
Mark Meddle		ARTHUR BOURCHIER.
Cool		CHARLES HAWTREY.
James		J. D. BEVERIDGE.
Martin		DENNIS EADIE.
Solomon Isaacs		WEEDON GROSSMITH.
Lady Gay Spanker . . .		IRENE VANBRUGH.
Grace Harkaway		PHYLLIS NEILSON TERRY.
Pert		MARIE TEMPEST.

The first night—March 4, 1841—found Covent Garden Theatre but half filled. The name of the author, "Mr. Lee Moreton," was unknown. During the performance he wandered about the lobby and corridors of the house, for he had been warned by Mme. Vestris to keep off the stage, as his presence would make the actors nervous. So he crept up into a back seat in the upper boxes, and there listened to his play. How slow it seemed, how bald! The first act provoked a little laughter here and there, and then he drew a breath. As the play proceeded, he discovered Mark Lemon, Douglas Jerrold and Gilbert à Becket seated together in the front row of an adjacent box. He crept into the row behind them and tried to overhear their opinions of the piece. When the situation came at the end of the act, Jerrold turned to his companions.

"That is fatal," he said; "he has reached his climax too early in the play. Nothing will go after that."

Lady Gay Spanker is the vital character of "London Assurance." Wellington never awaited the arrival of the Prussians at Waterloo with the pale anxiety that Boucicault waited for the entrance of Mrs. Nisbet. She came, she spoke, she conquered. When she described the hunt—in the grand speech of the play—she carried the house by storm. Jerrold, Lemon and à Becket rose in their seats and cheered. The pit seemed to boil over. Nothing was heard for several minutes.

Boucicault often described his emotions on that "first night." Late in life, when his fancy was mutinous, he was fond of romancing a bit. His story, as told above, almost in his own words, is probably over-colored, but it is at least picturesque. Then he goes on to tell how he paced Covent Garden up and down, back and forth, not caring where he directed his steps, until he found himself on Waterloo Bridge, seated in a recess, trying to cool his face by pressing it against the stone balustrade. It was raining, but he did not know it. Then there crept over him a dread that the end of the comedy might change the tide of success. He rose and hurried back to the theatre.

The fifth act was on; there was an ominous silence. Hush! Who is speaking? It was old Farren as *Sir Harcourt,* who, glancing askance at *Dazzle,* the adventurer, says, "Charles, who is Dazzle?"

"CHARLES—Dazzle? Well, I don't exactly know. I say, Dazzle, excuse an impertinent question.

"DAZZLE—Oh, certainly.

"CHARLES—Who are you?

"DAZZLE—I have not the slightest idea."

The house shook with peal after peal of laughter at the inimitable manner of Mathews. Every fibre of the young author quivered responsively. In a few moments after this the curtain descended. A strange uproar commenced—a din, amidst which it seemed impossible to discern what the audience wanted. In the midst of it all the author felt himself seized by some one, and presently he found himself behind the scenes, standing at the prompt entrance.

"Come," said Mathews, "don't you hear them calling for you?"

"For me!" he stammered. "What for?"

Mathews caught him by the arm, the stage manager pushed him forward, and he found himself suddenly in the presence of the audience.

Who can describe the feelings of this young Irishman, awkward in manner, short in stature, as he was brought down to the footlights and introduced as "Mr. Lee Moreton, the author of this comedy, ladies and gentlemen"![1]

After escaping from this ordeal, he stood amid the crowd of actors in the greenroom. Their faces beamed upon him as they poured compliments into his tingling ears. He stammered out something very incoherent to each of them. It was a great night for a mere stripling. Some of the critics sneered, indeed, the next morning, and among them Thackeray, who was not then great, but a somewhat obscure writer on "Fraser's" and other magazines. But "London Assurance," before very long, found a place among the moss-covered clas-

---

[1] It is scarcely worth while to dwell upon Boucicault's alleged indebtedness to John Brougham for collaboration in the authorship of "London Assurance." Lester Wallack, in his "Memories of the Last Fifty Years," remarks: "As to what Brougham had to do with the play, I have heard Boucicault on the point, and I have heard John Brougham himself on the point. There is very little doubt that Brougham first suggested the idea, and there is no doubt that he intended the part of *Dazzle* for himself. So far as I know, Mr. Brougham, for a certain sum of money, conceded to Mr. Boucicault his entire rights in the comedy. John was far less officious in the matter than his friends were. They invented all sorts of tales, but there is no question that the success of the whole thing was due to Mr. Boucicault, to his tact and cleverness, and to the brilliancy of his dialogue."

And, as Mr. Stephen Fiske sagely says: "The best proof that Boucicault alone was the author of 'London Assurance' is that he went on writing comedies like 'London Assurance,' but not quite so popular, such as 'The Irish Heiress' and 'Old Heads and Young Hearts,' while Brougham never wrote anything like it, his best comedy, 'Playing with Fire,' being in an entirely different style."

There is the gist and heart of the whole matter!

sics of English dramatic literature. It has shown, too, the same tenacity of stage life as "The Rivals" and "She Stoops to Conquer."

We could wish that Boucicault had curbed his exuberant fancy and that certain high-flown passages of rococo dialogue which have been the butt of all critics[1] from Thackeray down to Mr. A. D. Walkeley had been struck out by some friendly mentor of the precocious playwright. We must remember, however, that in 1841 rhodomontade *à la* Sheridan Knowles was regarded as superlatively brilliant, and sentiment of the Bulwer Lytton sort was not only relished in plays and novels, but actually affected in ordinary conversation. In 1841 the social institution known as "Tom and Jerryism"—*i.e.*, door-bell pulling, filching of doorknockers and changing of signs over the shops of tradesmen—still flourished among the young rakes of the town. Burgundy was the tipple immediately following breakfast. The fashionable entertainment was the ballet, not the opera. People might be arrested for debt, and duelling was still in fashion. Men wore white beaver hats, turn-over shirt-cuffs, military cloaks and satin waistcoats. The literary taste of the time found vent in "Keepsakes," "Beauty's Garlands" and like sentimental "annuals."

Finding the flowers and figures of speech of Bulwer Lytton so popular in all quarters, and

---

[1] "That despicable mass of inanity."—*Edgar Allan Poe* (1846), "The Literati" (Works, ed. Stedman and Woodberry, Vol. VIII, p. 31).

Sheridan Knowles's rhapsodies praised as gems of thought and feeling, the budding Boucicault took both of these luminaries as sure beacons to guide him to the harbor of popular success. They had stamped themselves upon his immaturity, and he easily absorbed their faults and their virtues.

What gave "London Assurance" the seal of popular approval, however, was the excellence of the characterization and the sure and skilful development of the story. Boucicault must have been born with the secret of stage construction.

Of all arts known to man, play-writing is one of the most difficult. Years of study, reading the plays of other men; years of apprenticeship on the stage, watching the work of the most expert actors and stage managers, will not suffice to impart the secret of the craft to one unblessed with stage instinct. Boucicault had the divine spark of the born playwright, and the success of "London Assurance" proved that he had done something more than catch the manner of the Restoration dramatists and their tawdry imitators; he had learned how to handle a dramatic motive surely and unerringly.

"The first object of the playwright," once remarked Dion, years afterward, "is to arouse interest; and the moment when that interest is felt, as soon as that crisis arrives, we know it instantly. The house is suddenly silenced, and we say, 'They 've caught it,' or 'We 've got it.' The author looks at the audience as his natural prey, and when he gets it in his power he does not relax his grip."

"London Assurance" seemed fair game for satire to Thackeray. His parody of the play is embedded in one of the chapters of "Sketches and Travels":

"It was one of Mr. Boyster's comedies of English life. Frank Nightrake and his friend, Bob Fitzoffley, appeared in the first scene, having a conversation with that impossible valet of English Comedy, whom many gentlemen would turn out of doors before he could get through half a length of the dialogue assigned. And as your true English Comedy is the representation of nature, I could not but think how like these figures on the stage and the dialogue which they used were to the appearance and talk of the English gentleman of the present day.

"The dialogue went on somewhat in the following fashion:

"Bob Fitzoffley (*Entering whistling.*) —The top of the morning to thee, Frank! What, at breakfast already? At chocolate and the morning toast, like a dowager of sixty? Slang! (*He pokes the servant with his cane.*) What has come to thy master, thou Prince of Valets! Thou pattern of Slaveys! Thou swiftest of Mercuries! Has the Honorable Francis Nightrake lost his heart or his head or his health?

"Frank (*Laying down the paper.*) —Bob, Bob, I have lost all three. I have lost my health, Bob, with thee and thy like over the Burgundy at the Club; I have lost my head, Bob, with thinking how I shall pay my debts; and I have lost my heart, Bob—oh, to such a creature!

"Bob—A Venus, of course?

"Slang—With the presence of Juno.

"Bob—And the modesty of Minerva.

"Frank—And the coldness of Diana.

"Bob—Pish! What a sigh is that about a woman! Thou shalt be Endymion, the nightrake of old, and conquer this shy goddess—hey, Slang?

"Herewith Slang takes the lead of the conversation, and propounds a plot for running away with the heiress; and I could not help remarking how like the comedy was to life—how the gentlemen always say 'thou' and 'prythee,' and 'go to,' and talk about heathen goddesses to each other; how their servants are always their particular intimates; how, when there is serious love-making between a gentleman and lady, a comic attachment invariably springs up between the valet and waiting-maid of each; how Lady Grace Gadabout, when she calls upon Rose Ringdove to pay a morning visit, appears in a low satin dress with jewels in her hair; how Saucebox, her attendant, wears diamond brooches and rings on all her fingers; while Mrs. Tallyho, on the other hand, transacts all the business of life in a riding-habit, and always points her jokes by a cut of the whip."

Boucicault was paid three hundred pounds for "London Assurance," and when it is remembered that Bulwer received the same for "The Lady of Lyons," and Sheridan Knowles was paid four hun-

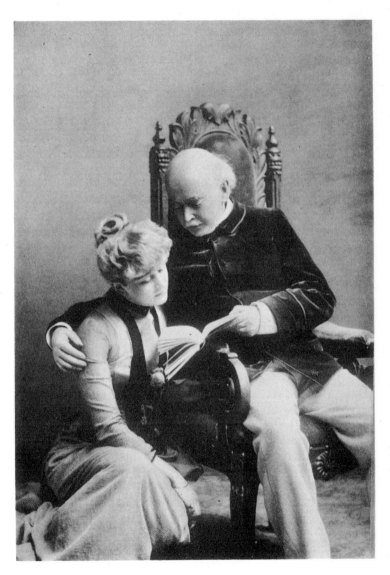

Dion Boucicault and Louise Thorndyke Boucicault

dred pounds for "The Love Chase," it was grand
recognition for a youth's play.[1]

[1] Mrs. Nisbet, who rollicked through *Lady Gay Spanker,*
was born Macnamara, and finished her career as Lady
Boothby. She was the successor on the English stage of
Mrs. Jordan, whose tradition she perpetuated. Her laugh
was a thing to ravish lovers, and brought suitors to her
feet. It was the most rippling, joyous and musical laugh
ever heard behind the footlights, and, repeated by the
echoes of the big theatre, it carried all hearers out into
the open and seemed a sound native to the open air.
Thackeray, so they said, fell head over ears in love with
her; and if the Fotheringay of the immortal "Pendennis"
was not inspired by Miss O'Neill, afterward Lady Wrixon
Beecher, she must have sat for her portrait in the person
of Mrs. Nisbet, who was wooed and won by Sir William
Boothby, Bart., of Ashbourne Hall, Derbyshire. Both
actresses had Irish forebears, both married titles and both
were personally acquainted with the author of "Pendennis." Desperately enamoured of Mrs. Nisbet—so the story
went in the greenroom of Covent Garden Theatre—
Thackeray sought in vain to win her hand. But she could
not conquer her aversion to the great one's broken nose,
and was indiscreet enough to say so; hence the none too
flattering portrait of Captain Costigan's daughter.

CHAPTER IV

*"Old Heads and Young Hearts," 1844—The condition
of the British dramatist previous to 1850—Free to
forage in France—Boucicault in Paris—His first
marriage and return to London—Dramatist and literary adviser for Charles Kean—Fecundity as an
adapter.*

ALL on fire with ambition, buoyant with pride
and hope was "Mr. Lee Moreton." Alas! the
playwright's lot, we are told, is full of wrath,
bitterness and disappointment.

Young Boucicault—he soon dropped the "Moreton" *nom de théâtre*—had many heartburnings
after his night of triumph. The critics descended,
hammer and tongs, on his next play, "The Irish
Heiress," produced under his own name at Covent
Garden, February 12, 1842. Neither the critics
nor the public showed much enthusiasm for "Alma
Mater," seen at the Haymarket on September 19
of the same year. Plays followed each other from
his pen with marvellous rapidity. He translated
French farces for a song—Charles Mathews drew
"Used Up."[1] He wrote comedies of society, which
society repudiated. He imitated first the Congreve
manner, then the Farquhar manner, and found

[1] Derived from "L'Homme Blasé." Acted by royal
command at Windsor Castle, January 4, 1849. Mathews
afterward put his own name on the bills as author.

34

them both hopelessly ineffective as a style of writing for modern audiences.

It looked as though his alpha was also to be his omega.

At last, after a couple of years of indefatigable labor and of trying to direct that labor profitably, he produced in "Old Heads and Young Hearts" another genuine success.[1]

He was in sore need of the money which this play brought him, for the triumph of "London Assurance" opened his extravagant heart, and nothing would serve him but he must have his mother and eldest brother over from Ireland to share the good fortune which seemed to be boundless. They consented to join him in London for a visit of six months. They remained twenty-five years. The boy was too proud of his burden to feel it, but the racehorse went to the plow with a little sigh as he put his neck in the collar to work for weekly wages. Sometimes he took a free gallop, as when he wrote "The School for Scheming" (Haymarket, February 4, 1847), and "Love in a Maze" (Princess's Theatre, March 6), but these five-act comedies added more to his literary than to his pecuniary credit.

"Old Heads and Young Hearts," however, was

---

[1] First acted at the Haymarket, November 18, 1844.
On the first night, when Charles Mathews, in the character of *Littleton Coke,* knelt to Mme. Vestris as *Lady Alice* and remarked, "I came to scoff, but I remain to pray," the audience mistook Goldsmith's line for a quotation from the Bible, and promptly hissed what they considered its flippant desecration.

an all-round success. It brought him money, and the friendship of Douglas Jerrold and Bulwer Lytton, and good words from all of his critics. Even Thackeray found the play praiseworthy. It is, indeed, one of Boucicault's best works. Yet because it is a wholly abstract view of life, it is the sort of play to awaken the lurking cynic in the soul of our modern critics. A comedy of types is apt to lose all relation to human nature; "Old Heads and Young Hearts" is purely a comedy of types.

The tastes of the theatregoers of one generation differ very widely from the tastes of the next generation. Nevertheless there are, in every period of taste, plays which, apart from their literary and dramatic value, all critics admit to possess, if not for themselves, then for sentimental associations, a strange, peculiar preciousness. These plays are revered, for curiosity, for tradition, for some connection they may have with the famous actors of the past.

In this category come "Old Heads and Young Hearts" and "London Assurance." For each new generation they put on a different aspect. The neophyte playgoer, with no respect for the classics of the stage and no sentiment for the past, takes Boucicault's first comedy for just what it is worth, measures it according to the amount of enjoyment it affords him. The sentimental playgoer—and he is not necessarily as old as Methuselah—looks at "London Assurance" through the lorgnette of 1841. The vanished past returns with each occasional "revival," and the shivering shades of Farren, Mrs. Nisbet, and Mathews people the stage in voiceless protest at the modern exponents of *Sir Harcourt, Lady Gay* and *Dazzle*. Poor ghosts!

At the last abortive revival of the play in New York, an English actor who appeared as *Meddle* failed to excite even the faintest ripple of mirth. He will go down in stage history, among actors, as the first *Meddle* who failed to "get a laugh."

To refute the charge of heartlessness and hollowness brought against "London Assurance," Boucicault showed that he could draw such a wholly admirable and lovable character as *Jesse Rural,* a type of simple and gentle goodness, of close kin to *Dr. Primrose,* the Vicar of Wakefield. Yet, in spite of this one genuine character, the play has a glittering hardness which suggested the remark that it was the work of an old heart and a young head. Clothed in the vesture of that Congreve drama which Boucicault had so well studied, "Old Heads and Young Hearts" has all the weaknesses of "The Double Dealer." Its world of self-conscious wits is no more real than the world of self-conscious psychologists in Mr. Henry James's novels. How refreshing to pass from it to the genial humanity of Goldsmith's "She Stoops to Conquer"!

Nevertheless the order of talent shown in "Old Heads and Young Hearts" was sufficient, under discipline and the self-denial of an artistic ambition, to have won Boucicault a lasting name in English dramatic literature. But the turning-point in the lane had come; he must now choose between two roads—one leading by showman Philistinism to popularity and prosperity, the other by æsthetic restraint and economy to honorable and permanent recognition as a dramatist. Boucicault obeyed the siren voices and went the road of the successful showman.

He should not be judged too harshly. Playwriting is a trade like another, and a young author soon grows weary of "sitting empty-stomached on Parnassus." Up to this time Boucicault had been painstaking; he had aspired; he had done his best to reconcile the irreconcilable. He had tried to wear two crowns: he had tried to play the double rôle of a literary artist and a popular purveyor to the theatre. It was an impossible task. The Elizabethan dramatists wrote under quite different conditions; if Greene, or Fletcher, or Shakespeare had stood in Boucicault's shoes at that precise moment when the tempter came, who knows but the same human yielding would have resulted?

A modern writer for the stage can never be a Carlyle; he can never be content to live on his conscience and a plate of oatmeal. To be clever always, and only occasionally to be true—that is the inevitable fate of the man who writes for the stage alone.

None the less, Boucicault had till then busied himself with literary form, the endeavor to observe with freshness and to record with charm. Now he saw that the race is not to the swift nor the battle to the strong, unless the swift and strong are crafty enough to draw the right weapons. And forthwith he became a popular playwright and a Philistine.

So Boucicault flung conscience and literary ambition overboard in order to become possessed of money and success. From the very first he showed a remarkable facility for appreciating what was best in others. The one character of *Jesse Rural* had proved him a master in the art of lifelike portraiture. But he ceased to be a creator, and was content to develop and improve the latent possibilities in the works of native bunglers and foreign adepts.

He was not a petty plagiarist; he did not lust for the fruits of other men's husbandry; he did not sneakingly pick the pocket of another man's reputation. Such degrading meannesses belong to the shysters of Grub Street. Boucicault was a literary swell; he was noble, magnanimous, splendid. Those who knew him best could not tell what he did with the money he made. His house in London was a little palace, himself a prince. "I am an emperor," he said, "and take what I think best for Art, whether it be a story from a book, a play from the French, an actor from a rival company."

This sounds like boasting; but Boucicault not only said it—he did it. He possessed an Aladdin's lamp, and he had only to rub it for a play to spring into being.

He levied on this writer or that. He took a lease of Scott and Dumas *père* for a certain season. He treated these authors precisely as people treat a house which they rent furnished, "the family

having left for Europe." He put a new plate
with a new name on the door, shifted the furniture
from one room to another, turned the conservatory
into a billiard-room. Thus the house for the time
being became his own, in spirit if not in truth.
And in Boucicault's case the landlord always remained abroad.

He would disembowel one author and recon-
stitute another. The process was not only laborious but it required skill. Boucicault worked at this
sort of production with unceasing energy. For
the architectural labors of authorship he showed
little inclination; but in the way of carpenter's
work and upholstering he was colossal. He found
it paid best.

"For example," he has told us in a magazine
article, "the usual price received by Sheridan
Knowles, Bulwer and Talfourd at that time for
their plays was £500. I was a beginner in 1841,
and received for my comedy 'London Assurance'
£300. For that amount the manager bought the
privilege of playing the work for his season. Three
years later I offered a new play to a principal London theatre. The manager offered me £100 for it.
In reply to my objection to the smallness of the
sum he remarked, 'I can go to Paris and select a
first-class comedy; having seen it performed, I feel
certain of its effect. To get this comedy translated
will cost me £25. Why should I give you £300 or
£500 for your comedy, of the success of which I
cannot feel so assured?' The argument was un-
answerable, and the result inevitable. I sold a

work for £100 that took me six months' hard work to compose, and accepted a commission to translate three French plays at £50 apiece. This work afforded me child's play for a fortnight. Thus the English dramatist of that day was obliged either to relinquish the stage altogether or become a French copyist."

Previous to 1850 the condition of the English dramatist resembled that of the author described in "Gil Blas," or of *Triplet* as depicted by Charles Reade in "Peg Woffington." The greater number of the literary men exercising this craft depended upon other means of livelihood. Planché was in a government office; Charles Dance held a clerkship in the Court of Bankruptcy; Robert Bell was editor of the "Atlas"; Talfourd was a serjeant-at-law; Bulwer was a man of large private property; Tom Taylor was a professor in a college; Mark Lemon kept a public-house; Douglas Jerrold struggled miserably till he became connected with "Punch"; Sheridan Knowles tried vainly to keep his head above water—he deserted the stage for the pulpit.

Boucicault, Madison Morton and Tom Robertson relied solely on the drama for an income. Boucicault was the first to strike his flag; he returned to the stage as an actor. Madison Morton went to pieces and died destitute. Tom Robertson endured for years such extremes of want—even of hunger—that his sufferings during this terrible period contributed largely to the cause of his early death.

For the four years between 1844 and 1848 Boucicault resided in Paris. Either tradition errs or he used the title of Viscount Boucicault. He made his headquarters at Meurice's, then as now one of the most fashionable hostelries in the French capital. As early as 1843 he entered into wedlock with a Frenchwoman some years his senior, and they went on a wedding tour in Switzerland. The loving pair started one day to cross a mountain, but only the husband came down on the other side. This, of course, is more or less legendary. But he turned up in London shortly after, dressed in the deepest mourning for his wife, who, according to the story he told, had fallen down a precipice in the Alps. There were not wanting people who ventured to hint that, perhaps, the husband had not been very anxious to attempt to rescue his wife; but these suspicions, as well as the whole story, could be verified by only one person—Boucicault himself. He was always reticent on the subject. This, said a wag, was his first successful adaptation from the French.

In 1848 we find him a petitioner in the Court of Bankruptcy, which elicited the information that his wife had left him £1000, and this he had not been long in spending.

About this time Macready, having abdicated the tragic throne in England, retired to private life. Charles Kean, who aspired to succeed to the throne of Macready, had assumed the management of the Princess's Theatre with a flourish of trumpets. He engaged Boucicault as his literary adviser and "right-hand man."

"Pauline" (Monday, March 17, 1851) and "The Corsican Brothers" (February 24, 1852) were two melodramas of Dumas *père*, reshaped by Boucicault, from whom Kean also received "Louis XI," adapted from Casimir Delavigne (Saturday, January 13, 1855; ran sixty-two nights), and "Faust and Marguerite" (April 19, 1854), adapted from Michel Carré.

Kean went to Paris to see Ligier in "Louis XI" and Fechter in "The Corsican Brothers" and "Pauline." He took it all in and returned top-full of these characters and the methods of the French actors. In after years, Henry Irving, at the instigation of Boucicault, took the rôle of *Louis XI* and played it, in Boucicault's opinion, with much more force than Kean; while in "The Corsican Brothers" Kean excelled Irving in the depth of his intensity. But it was all inspired by the French.

Other adaptations by Boucicault at about this period were: "The Willow Copse," from "La Closerie des Genêts," at the Adelphi, January 31, 1850; "The Broken Vow," from "L'Abbaye de Castro," produced at the Olympic, February 15, 1851; "The Queen of Spades," from Scribe's "La Dame de Pique," at the Olympic, April, 1851; "Geneviève," from Dumas's "Chevalier de la Maison Rouge," at the Adelphi, June, 1853; and "Janet Pride," from "Marie Jeanne, ou la Femme du Peuple," at the Adelphi, March 5, 1855.

Completely forgotten and out of date, all of

these plays have passed into the limbo of defunct things. With numberless other works of Boucicault and his contemporaries, they have found a dusty asylum on the shelves of Samuel French's play-publishing warehouse. Some of them might still serve as text-books to many modern play-wrights who, compared to Boucicault, are in constructive skill like bulls in a china-shop.

CHAPTER V

First appearance under his own name as an actor in London—An Irish vampire—Meets Agnes Robertson—Her early career as a child singer and juvenile actress—Falls in love with Boucicault—Their departure for New York.

ON June 14, 1852, at the Princess's Theatre, Boucicault made what has generally been chronicled as his début on the London boards under his own name.[1] He assumed the title rôle in his own play "The Vampire." Charles Kean deemed "vampires" beneath his tragic dignity; so Boucicault himself appeared as the supernatural creature who could only be brought back to a corporeal state again by being laid in the "moonbames" on the heights of Snowdon. Oddly enough, Boucicault's brogue, which always came out strong except in French dialect parts, did not seem anachronistic. Vampires, forsooth, may be classed as cosmopolites, not being indigenous to any particular clime. The play, an altogether weird and dreadful thing, was announced on the bills as

[1] His actual London début was at the Haymarket, Saturday, March 9, 1839, when he appeared, under the name of "Lee Moreton," as *Tim Donoghue* in his own farce "Lodgings to Let." A play-bill of this performance is owned by Mr. Alfred Becks, at one time a secretary for Boucicault.

a "spectral drama in three dreams." Its plot was reminiscent of an old play in which T. P. Cooke[1] thrilled and delighted his followers and, for the nonce, turned the theatre into a "Chamber of Horrors." Boucicault enacted the "monster" with due paleness of visage, stealthiness of pace and solemnity of tone. But for some reason or other, the fantastical horrors of the thing served only to weary the spectators, and those who came to shudder remained to yawn.

A rather better fate attended his next work, "The Prima Donna," a pretty little sentimental comedy (produced September 18, 1852) which ran for thirty-four nights.

In Charles Kean's company was a young actress of striking beauty and unusual talent who was destined to be the second Mrs. Boucicault.

This was Miss Agnes Robertson, the protégé and ward of the Keans. Born in Edinburgh on Christmas Day, 1833, the daughter of Thomas Robertson of that city, she came before the public at an early age, first as a child singer at Aberdeen, next as a precocious actress at the age of ten in "The Spoiled Child," and afterwards at Hull with the Terry family. At seventeen she was at Glasgow, and she is known to have sung in public in Dublin, at Judd's music-hall, Grafton Street. The

---

[1] The T. P. Cooke "Vampire" was first disclosed in 1820, and revived in 1829, both times at the English Opera House. Boucicault afterward changed the name of his play to "The Phantom," but it still proved impotent to draw.

site is now Messrs. Millar and Beatty's carpet-store.[1]

A few years later, in January, 1851, she made her first appearance in London as a page in "A Wife's Secret" at the Princess's Theatre, then under the management of Mr. and Mrs. Charles Kean. She also played *Nerissa* in "The Merchant of Venice." She advanced rapidly, playing the light comedy parts with a girlish ingenuousness that charmed the Kean *clientèle*.

In "The Prima Donna" the character of *Margaret* was expressly written to suit her delicate style. Author and actress forthwith fell in love. She thrust aside a coronet offered her by the Earl of Hopetown to take the hand of the debonair Dion. It is a pity the sacrifice was not better rewarded.

Some slight difference arising between Charles Kean and Boucicault induced him to relinquish his position in the Princess's Theatre, and in September, 1853, he sailed for New York.[2]

[1] The late ex-Chancellor (Rev. Dr.) Tisdall vouched for this. He had had a lifelong experience of the Dublin stage and wrote many essays on various theatrical subjects for "The Era."

[2] His fame had preceded him. Several of his plays had already found fashionable favor at the Park, Wallack's and Burton's Chambers Street theatres. "London Assurance" had been seen at the Park as early as October 11, 1841, when Charlotte Cushman, the first *Lady Gay Spanker* in America, gave a serious and constrained rendering of the part that was absurdly inappropriate. "Old Heads and Young Hearts" was acted December 2, 1844, simultaneously at two theatres—the Park and the Bowery.

CHAPTER VI

Début of Agnes Robertson at Burton's Theatre, New York — Her extraordinary success in Boston — Extended tour of the United States — A pen picture of New York in 1856 — "The Poor of New York" — "Jessie Brown; or, The Relief of Lucknow" — Boucicault opens a theatre in Washington.

O N the 22d of October, 1853, the bills of Burton's Theatre informed the public of New York that Miss Agnes Robertson would make her first appearance in the United States. She had arrived in Canada a few months before, and had appeared in Montreal. Boucicault, who sailed on a later steamer, joined her in New York (September 18, 1853); and although their marriage was not publicly announced, it was understood among their confrères of the greenroom, at least, that they were man and wife. Miss Robertson made her début at Burton's in "The Young Actress," a musical interlude by Boucicault, altered from an old piece. After three months in New York, where she had gathered around her a host of admirers, she went to Boston, in January, 1854, for an engagement at the Boston Museum. The excitement caused by her performances spread throughout the city and environs; it gained the neighboring villages and towns of New England, and special trains were

48

run for the first time to bring hundreds to witness the performances of the actress. The engagement was prolonged from two to four weeks, then to six, and subsequently to eight weeks. Old Bostonians who recall these appearances say that the furore was beyond all precedent. The tickets of admission were sold at a premium of five and six dollars each, and at her benefit the last night of her engagement the applicants for seats blocked up the access to the theatre and the street in front. The overjoyed manager of the Museum, Moses Kimball, induced Miss Robertson to prolong her engagement for the ninth week, and within four hours, such was the crowd, every seat in the theatre was bought up for the ensuing week. The enthusiasm created by Agnes Robertson among the women of Boston was so great that her promenades through the streets were beset with crowds who followed her from place to place. The corridors of the Tremont House, where she resided, were blocked up with fair admirers, who almost invaded her apartments. The childlike grace and modesty of manner with which she received all these honors that fell so suddenly and thickly upon her won more hearts to her cause than the exquisite power of her acting on the stage. Mr. Kimball, the manager, netted something like $20,000 on the engagement.

From Boston, Miss Robertson went to Washington, Philadelphia, Chicago and other cities. At New Orleans, in 1855, she appeared as *Violet* in "The Life of an Actress," in which Boucicault himself sustained the eccentric rôle of *Grimaldi* with marked success.[1]

In 1856 they were back in New York.

It must have been a curious city at that epoch. "It was not a city," records Boucicault in a magazine article. "It was a theatre. It was a huge fair. Bunting of all nationalities, and of no nationality, was flaunting over the streets. Poles of liberty accentuated the 'rights of man.' Bands of music preceded processions of ragged boys bearing flags and tattered banners. Irish was spoken at the wharves, German in the saloons, French in the restaurants. But the chiefest feature of this polyglot city was its boyhood—a boy in heart, but a man, and a very shrewd man, in head."

Curious and quick about the new world, Bouci-

[1] Mr. and Mrs. E. A. Sothern, Dyott, George Holland and Mrs. Vernon were in the cast. This play was produced in London at the Adelphi on March 1, 1862. "Mr. Boucicault's portraiture of the by turns obsequious, courteous and indignant *Grimaldi* was in all respects a masterpiece of histrionic ability. What is technically called 'make-up' was complete; and his manner throughout was true to the natural bearing of a man fallen into misfortune, but conscious of noble birth and noble feelings. He showed, too, some extraordinary powers. While teaching his pupil, he has to point out to her how Rachel delivered a particular speech, and finds it necessary to resort to the original French. This feat he brilliantly accomplished. His nervous anxiety for his débutante's success on the stage, and his passionate disappointment when he misses her from the next scene and learns the story of her abduction, were both admirably delineated. These things place Mr. Boucicault in the front rank as an artist of versatile abilities and a comprehensive mind."—*The Athenæum,* London, March 8, 1862.

cault was surprised to find the American theatres superior in every respect to the theatres in England. The plays were better acted. He had left behind him in London no such comedians as Blake, Burton, Walcot, Holland, Lester Wallack and Laura Keene. The great school of pantomime, which became extinct in London after the death of Grimaldi, flourished in the United States under the Ravels.[1] Neither the press nor the public seemed to recognize this artistic wealth. They had been taught subjection to London and to Paris in all such matters, and willingly accepted their inferiority. They had no drama of native growth. They had no laws protecting copyright in the performance of dramatic works. The casual contributions to American dramatic literature from George Boker, Dr. Bird and others were *publici juris;* any one was at liberty to perform them freely. In the presence of such an impediment the existence of an American drama was impossible. It required three years to remove it. In 1856 Boucicault succeeded in getting Congress to pass a brief statute investing the author of a drama or the composer of a musical work, in addition to the

---

[1] Gabriel, Antoine, Jerome and François Ravel toured America for more than a score of years, returning to their native town in France—Toulouse—with a well-won harvest of American dollars. They were most accomplished mimes, and their repertoire of pantomimes ran the gamut of their art from the broadly comic to the tragic. Associated with them at various times were the Lehmans, the Martinettis, Blondin, Mme. Yrca Matthias and Leon Javelli. Their troupe was a polyglot assemblage of the pantomimic geniuses of all nations.

sole right of printing and publishing, with the sole right also of representing it or permitting it to be represented.

Boucicault had used these three years in the study of the American people, their tastes and the direction of their dramatic appetites. Accompanying his wife on her starring engagements in the principal cities, he saw many sections of the country.[1] He was a shrewd observer, receiving impressions with the alertness of a sympathetic intellect, and pigeonholing them for future use like the practical playwright he was.

First of all, he tried his luck as a lecturer and a reader—Dickens and Thackeray, not to mention Dr. Dionysius Lardner, were getting gold in heaps at this sort of thing. Boucicault favored an unappreciative audience with a series of "Winter Evenings" at Hope Chapel; they were so wintry that people preferred sitting by their own fires, instead of trusting to the precarious warmth of Boucicaultian genius.[2]

[1] Boucicault's first American appearance as an actor occurred November 10, 1854, at the Broadway Theatre, as *Sir Charles Coldstream* in "Used Up." It was in this same rôle—and at the same theatre, by the way—that Lester Wallack had made his American début on September 27, 1847. The old Broadway Theatre stood on the east side of Broadway, between Pearl and Anthony streets, the latter now called Worth Street.

[2] The subjects of the lectures were: "Sketches of European Society," "Woman, Her Rights (?) and Her Wrongs," "My Literary Life; or, The Vicissitudes of a Man of Letters in London and Paris," and "The Story

The American stage was in a transitory state.
Tragedy was dying a slow death under Edwin
Forrest, just as it was in England under Charles
Kean. Romantic drama and epigrammatic comedy
had lost all charm; the actual, the local, the con-
temporaneous, alone seemed to interest the public.
And one day, while looking over the pictures of a
magazine, Boucicault thought it might be worth
while to take the events of the day into partnership
with him.

First he turned out "The Poor of New York,"
a superficial but graphic picture of events transpir-
ing about the time of the financial panic of 1857.

The play had a long and successful run at Wallack's Theatre, and Lester Wallack, then known as
Mr. Lester, became the prime favorite of the town
through his popular performance of *Tom Badger*.
Often as "The Poor of New York" has been revived, it always makes an appeal to an audience,
the secret being that it is a human play, and shows

of the Stage." He also read his then unacted version of
"Louis XI."

In spite of his success as a playwright, the public
could not be persuaded to accept him as a lecturer, even
though he faithfully promised to initiate them, as it were,
into the mysteries of London fashionable life and tell
them piquant stories about the living originals from whom
he drew the characters of *Sir Harcourt Courtly, Dazzle,*
and *Lady Gay Spanker*. He read his lectures to empty
benches. The public either did not put confidence in his
alluring promises or did not care to be made a party to
the stupendous social secrets which he proposed to dis-
close.

us how, among the poorest and lowliest, kindliness and charity are always to be found.

Encouraged by this success, Boucicault tackled bigger game. The Sepoy Rebellion was a thrilling subject to the public mind. The news of the massacre at Cawnpore had filled the world with horror; the heroism of Lucknow had made the newspapers romantic. A petty Hindoo squireen had contrived to swindle and murder himself into a ghastly notoriety; a small garrison of Europeans were shut up in Lucknow, besieged by an overwhelming force of natives; Jessie Brown, a young Scottish girl, had kept the garrison from surrender by proclaiming, with the fire of Joan of Arc, that the pibroch of a Scottish regiment coming to their relief was ringing in her ears. If one pauses for a moment to think what terrible and noble realities of anguish, despair, courage, faith, suffering and strength are shut up in that single word—Lucknow—it will not be pleasant to reflect upon the processes of mind which wrought the story into a stage show. But Dion Boucicault produced "Jessie Brown; or, The Relief of Lucknow," and was crowned with laurel that same night (February 22, 1855). Wallack's Theatre was given over to tom-toms, khitmutgars, sowars, spleuchans, pipes, tartans, and all the mingled paraphernalia of an East Indian spectacle. He himself acted the merciless Sepoy. Nobody else in Wallack's company would consent to play the part. In London, where a dramatization of the episode had also been made, the unhappy individual who represented Nana

Sahib had been dealt with, not according to his histrionic skill, but according to the merits of his "principal," and provoked such storms of wrath and fury from pit and gallery that the stage became a kind of beleaguered fortress and the play was carried on under a shower of missiles. Not only the traditional and harmless orange-peel, but sticks, bottles, umbrellas, and apprentices' caps rained upon the miserable rajah whenever he made his appearance, and at the close the manager was obliged to carry him away, "like the monarchy of July," in a cab from the threatened violence of a mob assembled outside the stage door. Small wonder, then, that every actor in New York refused to risk his life in playing the part.

With splendid audacity, Boucicault stepped into the breach and himself personated the "Demon of Cawnpore." When he strolled down to the footlights, with his carcanet of brilliants, his rustling tunic, his walnut physiognomy, and a magnificent pair of moustachios, the gallery held its breath in awe and threw nothing at him.[1]

[1] Never moderate in praise of himself, Boucicault delighted in writing the "ads." for the newspapers, thereby acquainting the world with the worth of his services. He usually found a fresh supply of superlatives to boom every new play from his pen. The production of "Jessie Brown," for example, was preceded by florid proclamations, declaring him to be the "only author now living, of the English drama, whose works have withstood that truest and greatest of all critics—Time."

Such inferior luminaries as Sir Edward Bulwer Lytton and James Sheridan Knowles, both alive at the time, must have suffered a common eclipse.

Not so the brave John Brougham. He was then con-

"Pauvrette" and "The Pope of Rome" (both produced at Niblo's in October, 1858) were skilful adaptations from the French. They served to mark farther advances in Agnes Robertson's art, but did not have any emphatic success.

On January 6, 1858, in partnership with William

nected with a rival theatre—Burton's—and his benefit being near at hand, he burst forth into an eloquent pæan of self-praise which far transcended Boucicault's dithyrambic rapture in audacious brilliancy of invention and in the reckless sublimity of its appeal to the finer feelings of our nature. I cannot resist the temptation to rescue it from the ephemeral journals of 1859 and embalm it in the perdurable pages of this book:

"ASTOUNDING ANNOUNCEMENT. MR. BROUGHAM hereby makes known to his million of enthusiastic admirers in all quarters, that, inasmuch as HIS BENEFIT is appointed to take place on Thursday evening next, February 25, he thinks it a favorable opportunity to BLOW HIS OWN TRUMPET, knowing full well that if he does not nobody else will, and, philosophically considered, he also begs to insinuate that as there is no individual alive who has a better opinion of the subscriber than he fortunately possesses of himself, he is determined no longer to hide his AMAZING LITERARY BLAZE UNDER A BUSHEL, but boldly announces himself as the ONLY LIVING DRAMATIST out of the dead languages, whose brilliant though slightly appreciated ability ought to be the BEACON OF THE AGE. With characteristic diffidence, he simply appends the great and ABSORBING PUBLIC FACT that upon the occasion alluded to he will present an ARRAY OF IMPOSING ATTRACTIONS hitherto unequaled in the HISTRIONIC ANNALS OF THE WORLD, and interpreted by a STUNNING CONSTELLATION OF SUPERHUMAN SPLENDOR. He will gratify and indulge the public with a fragmentary collection from the prodigiously popular productions emanating from his own UNPARALLELED PEN; and, for fear that their effects should be too overpowering, alloy their AURIFEROUS

Stuart,[1] Boucicault opened a new theatre in Washington, D. C., which they converted out of an old dancing saloon known as "Carusi's."   J. B. Howe,[2] who was engaged as leading man, has related some interesting anecdotes pertinent to the Boucicaults:

"In the train which had taken me from Boston I saw a sweet, modest, arch-looking little lady, with a pretty blue-eyed babe in her lap, and by her side a coloured nurse, and do all I could, I never succeeded in taking my eyes from her, except when she now and then caught me in the act; and, to my surprise, when I entered the so-called theatre on the same evening, to see what sort of place it was, and ascertain what time the call would be on the morrow, as we were to open three nights after, I saw the same nurse and the same baby, but the mother was absent.   When I inquired of the coloured girl, 'Who claimed the child?' she gave a grin and answered, 'I does.'

" 'You are not its mother?'

" 'Lar' bress you, no. Dar 's her mudder.'

"And she pointed to the form of the beautiful creature whom I subsequently learned was Miss Agnes Robertson.   I was introduced to her shortly

GRANDEUR with two or three less meritorious concoctions from UNDISTINGUISHED SOURCES. N. B. —This will be pluter-positively the absolutely last appearance of the above mentioned MULTIFARIOUSLY ACCOMPLISHED POETICO-PHILOSOPHICAL AUTHOR-ACTOR AND SOLE, SELF-PATENTED DRUMMOND LIGHT OF DRAMATIC LITERATURE."

[1] A journalist and manager. Real name, O'Flaherty.
[2] "The Cosmopolitan Actor," 1887.

afterwards by Dion Boucicault, who was up to his eyes in business, nailing lace curtains to the private boxes, in which I assisted him.

"There was a call for that night, but as some of the company had not put in an appearance yet, it was dismissed, and we met next morning to rehearse 'The Life of an Actress' and 'Milly the Milkmaid,' in which I was included as *Arthur Shafton* and *Algernon*.

"The success of the two stars was assured at once, and the whole of that summer season the seats were sold days in advance. So great was the rage to see the fairy star, as she was called—and she was really like a fairy—that crowds would assemble on Pennsylvania Avenue and present bouquets to her as she passed along from her hotel to the theatre.

"I was with them about ten weeks, playing all the juveniles, until I left to go for the leading business to H. C. Jarrett, lessee of the Baltimore Museum; and before I bid them farewell let me relate an instance of the thorough business instinct and professional impartiality of one whom I consider the greatest writer and adapter of modern drama in the world, and one of the finest character actors on the stage. On the morning of the rehearsal of 'The Life of an Actress,' Miss Agnes Robertson failed to do a little bit of business of kneeling and falling at the feet of the gentleman who played the heavy part, and Dion asked her to do it again. Agnes did it again, but in the same manner as before.

" 'No, no; that won't do,' said Dion. 'Can't you rise slowly from your chair, giving the audience the idea that you are still under the influence of the narcotic? Grasp the corner of the table, so, and, as if fearing to fall, you still retain your hold on the table until your left knee touches the ground; then is the time to seize Mr. Ralston's right hand with your left, so, and you turn gently round and fall in the centre at his feet.'

" 'I know that, Dion dear, but is there any necessity for me to do all that now? I 've played the part before.'

" 'I know that, but not with the present members. I want *them* to see what you are going to do; go back, please. Please, Mr. Ralston, once more, to oblige Mrs. Boucicault. Now, if you please.'

"But the sweet little creature did not please. She burst into tears, and Dion exclaimed, 'Never mind, ladies and gentlemen; dismiss the rehearsal.' That was all; we dispersed, and, need I say, in the most elegant confusion."

Besides appearing here in all the plays of their varied repertoire, Boucicault essayed the rôle of *Havresac,* the Napoleonic veteran, in his capital little drama "Napoleon's Old Guard," Agnes Robertson playing the daughter, *Mélanie.*

CHAPTER VII

Partnership with William Stuart at the Winter Garden, New York — Joseph Jefferson their comedian — Boucicault's astuteness at rehearsals — His masterly stage-craft — Agnes Robertson's gift for pathos — Success of "The Octoroon" — Its tactful treatment of the slavery question — Jefferson's hit as Salem Scudder.

A GRACEFUL homage is that paid Boucicault by Joseph Jefferson in his delightful "Auto-biography," wherein he tells of his first appearance as *Caleb Plummer*.

This was at the Winter Garden, New York, in the fall of 1859. The theatre was under the joint direction of William Stuart and Boucicault. A strong company had been secured, and Mr. Jefferson was the leading comedian.

The opening play (September 14) was Bouci-cault's adaptation of Dickens's "Cricket on the Hearth," rechristened "Dot."

"Previous to the commencement of the season," narrates Mr. Jefferson, "Mr. Boucicault and I had some conversation in relation to the opening bill. I told him I was rather apprehensive of my hitting the part of *Caleb Plummer,* as I had never acted a character requiring pathos, and, with the exception of the love scene in 'Our American Cousin,' as yet had not spoken a serious line upon the stage.

He seemed to have more confidence in my powers than I had, and insisted that I could act the part with success. I agreed, therefore, to open in *Caleb,* with the understanding that I should finish the performance with a farce, so in the event of my failing in the first piece, I might save my reputation in the last. He assented to the arrangement, but warned me, however, that I would regret it; and he was right, for when the curtain fell upon 'Dot,' I should have much preferred not to have acted in the farce. So the little piece was taken off after the first night, as I was quite satisfied with *Caleb* alone.

"An incident occurred during the first rehearsal of 'Dot' that may be worth relating, as it bears upon a theory in acting that I have established for myself ever since it took place. Mr. Boucicault, I think, understood me, and felt from what I had said to him on previous occasions that I was not averse to suggestions in the dramatic art, and was in the habit of listening to advice, though I always reserved to myself the right of acting on my own judgment as to whether the proffered counsel was good or bad. During my rehearsal of the first scene, which I went through just as I intended acting it at night, I saw by his manner that he was disappointed with my rendering of the part, and I asked him what was the matter. He replied, 'If that is the way you intend to act the part, I do not wonder you were afraid to undertake it.' This was a crushing blow to a young man from one older in years and experience; but feeling that there was something to learn, I asked him to explain what he meant. 'Why, you have acted your last scene first; if you begin in that solemn strain, you have nothing left for the end of the play.' This was his remark, or words to the same effect; and I am certainly indebted to him, through this advice, for whatever success I achieved in the part.

"I am not sure whether Mr. Boucicault was aware of what a large field for dramatic thought he opened up; and if I did not clearly understand the importance of it then, I have found it out since, and, so far as I have been able, applied it as a general rule. These reflections taught me never to anticipate a strong effect; in fact, to lead your audience by your manner, so that they shall scarcely suspect the character capable of such emotion; then, when some sudden blow has fallen, the terrible shock prepares the audience for a new and striking phase in the character; they feel that under these new conditions you would naturally exhibit the passion which till then was not suspected."

This tribute to Boucicault's stagecraft, coming from so accomplished an artist as Jefferson, seems to me the solidest compliment that one great actor could pay to another.

An adaptation of Scribe's "L'Ours et le Pacha," and described by a critic of the day as a ridiculous piece of buffoonery, called "Chamooni the Third," introduced Mr. Jefferson and another first-rate actor, "Tom" Johnston, in burlesque rôles, in which they were called upon to disguise themselves

as a pair of polar bears. The affair was short-
lived.

Dickens was again laid under contribution, and
a skilful dramatization of "Nicholas Nickleby"
was next produced. As *Newman Noggs,* Jefferson shared honors with Boucicault, who made a
very volatile *Mantalini,* and with Agnes Robertson,
who impersonated *Smike.* We can gain some idea
of the peculiar pathos of Miss Robertson's acting
from the following bit of appreciative criticism by
a writer of that day:

"Her voice is of itself a plea for pity. It is most
musical, most melancholy, and in uttering the wandering fancies of *Smike's* crushed and broken
spirit it falls upon the ear as the words of Dickens
do upon the heart, like 'sweet bells jangled out of
tune,' yet something less than 'harsh.'"

Pathos of the simple, old-fashioned ballad style
was the strongest gift in Miss Robertson's endowment of talents. In voice, in face, in gesture, she
moved upon the stage, the song of "Auld Robin
Gray" in living female shape. She proved, too, as
Smike, as *Jeanie Deans,* and as *Jessie Brown,* her
delicate appreciation of the moods which produce
excessive exaltation or depression in very sensitive
organisms; and she could simulate the half-mad-
ness either of inspiration or of despair in such na-
tures with rare felicity.

But the triumphant success of the year 1859 for
Boucicault, when Jefferson's fortunes were linked
with his and Agnes Robertson's, was "The Octo-

roon,"[1] most virile of antebellum plays. The slavery question was on everybody's tongue. He could not have chosen a more inflammatory topic.

Coming at a time when the most intense feeling prevailed in the United States between the Abolitionists and the partisans of slavery, the announcements preceding "The Octoroon" heightened the excitement. The Mississippi was to flow through the play, which was described as a picture of the river-world of that day. The very name "Octoroon" was an emotion. What word could better hide a plot, a privy conspiracy of sedition and anarchy! Surely here was abundant material to feed the flames that were soon to burst into a conflagration between North and South. But instead of manufacturing mischief, Boucicault treated his subject in the most impartial way. The hottest and loyalest Southerner, viewing the play with an equable eye, could find in it nothing that the most popular of Southern authors or authoresses of the day might not have written. Mr. Simms of South Carolina might have sketched the Indian, the lynchers, the canebrakes and river-sweeps; Miss Marion Harland of Virginia might have limned the home life of the Atalcapas negroes and their affectionate masters. There can be no doubt, of

[1] Produced December 9, at the Winter Garden, seven days after John Brown's soul went marching on ahead of Emancipation.

Dion Boucicault as *Conn* in "The Shaughraun"

course, that Boucicault had the slavery question in his eye when he wrote "The Octoroon," just as he had the Sepoy mutiny in the same organ when he wrote "Jessie Brown," and the financial crisis of 1857 when he put "The Poor of New York" upon the stage. But he solved the difficult problem of portraying Southern life upon the stage without offending sensitive Southerners or overheating truculent Northerners, and he combined truth with picturesqueness.

"The Octoroon" is curious and interesting as a document of the day. Be it noted that Boucicault had been in the United States for a comparatively few years when he wrote the play. With what ready sympathy he caught the spirit and feeling of the times, and with what graphic skill reproduced American habits of thought and speech upon the stage!

Zoe, the "octoroon," is the daughter of a quadroon slave by her white owner and master; hence her mystical designation. She is likewise a slave, and is therefore exposed for sale; and is also unfortunate enough to have fallen in love with a youth of pure Caucasian blood. And all this passes in Louisiana and is set forth with all the pomp and circumstance of veranda-shaded houses; slave sales; kindly, prosperous Southern planters; rascally Northern overseers plotting incredible villainy; gallant Creole gentlemen loving justice and mercy; leather-legged Indian; explosive high-pressure steamboats and lurid cotton conflagrations.[1]

Joseph Jefferson, who played the Yankee overseer, *Salem Scudder,* with inimitable effect, tells us in his "Autobiography" how Southerners and Northerners left the Winter Garden convinced that Boucicault had, in writing the play, sympathized with their respective causes. Makers of mischief who found fire, fury and fanatical vengeance in the title as they would in the curve of a cat's tail or the wink of a white owl's eye, praised "The Octoroon" to the skies. Dealing with the all-absorbing subject of slavery, it was, as Mr. Jefferson says, "produced at a dangerous time. The slightest allusion to this now banished institution only served to inflame the country, which was already at a white heat. The drama, told so well, had a great effect on the audience, for there was at this time a divided feeling in New York with regard to the coming struggle. Some were in favor of war, others thought it best to delay and, if pos-

---

[1] The cast was as follows:

Salem Scudder	JOSEPH JEFFERSON.
Jacob M'Closky	T. B. JOHNSTON.
Sunnyside	GEORGE HOLLAND.
George Peyton	A. H. DAVENPORT.
Lafouche	J. H. STODDART.
Wah-no-tee	DION BOUCICAULT.
Captain Ratts	HARRY PEARSON.
Pete	GEORGE JAMIESON.
Paul	IONE BURKE.
Zoe	AGNES ROBERTSON.
Dora Sunnyside	MRS. J. H. ALLEN.
Mrs. Peyton	MRS. W. R. BLAKE.

sible, avert it; and it was deemed unwise, if not culpable, by many for us to act 'The Octoroon' at such a time. Then there were various opinions as to which way the play leaned—whether it was Northern or Southern in its sympathy. The truth of the matter is, it was non-committal. The dialogue and characters of the play made one feel for the South, but the action proclaimed against slavery and called loudly for its abolition. When the old negro, just before the slave sale, calls his colored 'bedrin' around him and tells them they must look their best so as to bring a good price for the 'missis,' and then, falling on his knees, asks a blessing on the family who had been so kind to them, the language drew further sympathy for the loving hearts of the South; but when they felt by the action of the play that the old darkey who had made them weep was a slave, they became Abolitionists to a man.

"When *Zoe,* the loving octoroon, is offered to the highest bidder, and a warm-hearted Southern girl offers all her fortune to buy *Zoe* and release her from the threatened bondage awaiting her, the audience cheered for the South; but when again the action revealed that she could be bartered for, and was bought and sold, they cheered for the North as plainly as though they had said, 'Down with slavery!' This reveals at once how the power of dramatic action overwhelms the comparative impotency of the dialogue."

The most novel incident in the play is undoubtedly the murder of little *Paul* and the accidental photographing of this event. It thrilled the audience, but it did not spring from the brain of Boucicault. It is found in "The Filibuster," by Albany Fonblanque, a novel that appeared that same year, published by Ward & Locke, Fleet Street, London. The chapter containing the episode is entitled "The Sun Picture."

If you want to get the full measure of Boucicault's talent, read the delectable scenes of *Old Pete* in "The Octoroon." He is far more genuine and human than *Uncle Tom* or any other negro in fiction that preceded him. Lordly, unctuous, sun-warmed, and much petted, *Pete* is the "ole nigger" of a good Southern family. Sure of his status, such as it was,—a fact and not an uncertainty,—submissive and despotic by turns, but full of quick, kindly, affectionate impulses; a law and an authority among his fellow servants, and a "daddy" to the children of his master, whose place none can dispute,—this was the type that Boucicault originated in 1859, and which has since been lovingly elaborated by Joel Chandler Harris and Thomas Nelson Page.

The actor who impersonated *Old Pete* in "The Octoroon" was George Jamieson, once associated with Edwin Forrest and the innocent victim of Forrest's insensate jealousy at the time of his celebrated divorce.[1] Boucicault thought so highly of Jamieson and his acting of *Old Pete* that, later, he

[1] Killed by an express train while walking on the railroad tracks near his home at Glenmont, New York, October 3, 1868.

took him with him to London for the production
there of "The Octoroon." Jamieson was never surpassed in the part, although actors like W. J.
LeMoyne and Charles Walcot scored in it. His
indignant protest at the slave sale, when he found
he was going cheap, was a bit of acting that never
failed to tell; and following, as it did, the little
speech which he made to the other slaves, exhorting them to appear well at the sale so as to bring
good prices, it touched all hearts.

The picturesque part of the Indian, *Wah-no-tee*,
was first enacted by Boucicault himself, with a
wealth of pantomimic detail. It is, in theatrical
parlance, a "pantomime part," and has been effec-
tively played by pantomimists like Christopher J.
Smith in London, and James S. Maffitt, Tony
Denier and Fred A. Stone, of Montgomery and
Stone, in America.

CHAPTER VIII

*The Boucicaults transfer their services to Laura Keene
— Production of "The Colleen Bawn" — The true
story of Eily O'Connor, upon which Gerald Griffin
based his novel—Boucicault's admirable originality in
dramatizing Griffin's work—Success of the play in
New York, London, Dublin and Paris— The novelty
of the water-cave scene.*

A DISAGREEMENT between Boucicault and
his partner, William Stuart, and a flare-up
between Agnes Robertson and Mrs. John Hoey
brought the engagement of the Boucicaults at the
Winter Garden to an abrupt end. They lost no
time in moving, bag and baggage, to Laura
Keene's Theatre, where they opened in "The Trial
of Effie Deans," a dramatization of "The Heart of
Midlothian." This was followed by a new comedy
called "Vanity Fair" (not in any way related to
Thackeray's immortal work), upon which they relied to finish a prosperous season. The play proved
a speedy and ghastly failure. Disaster lay ahead,
in which all the profits of the season—and more,
too—must inevitably disappear. Boucicault's fertility was at a standstill; his facile Muse had
deserted him; his mine of ideas seemed to be ex-
hausted. As a last resort he looked to his own
beloved country for inspiration. The answer came
in "The Colleen Bawn."

The story of this epoch-making success has been told with great complacency by the author, and if we did not know of his love for romancing, we might give it credence.

"Have you nothing? No subject—no play half written? Can you think of nothing to replace this unlooked-for collapse?" pleaded Laura Keene, after the failure of "Vanity Fair."

"I have nothing," answered Boucicault. "Let us meet to-morrow and talk it out."

It was a bitter night, he goes on romantically, and the sleet, driven by a northern blast, lashed his face as he turned down the alley from the stage door. A few steps from the theatre, a dim lamp in a cellar showed a thrifty little Italian who sold old books. Descending into the den [*sic*], Boucicault picked out a dozen cheap novels at hazard, and, with the pockets of his overcoat stuffed with them, went home to spend the hours of the night in searching them for a play. The following morning Laura Keene received this note: "I have it! I send you seven steel engravings of scenes around Killarney. Get your scene-painter to work on them at once. I also send a book of Irish melodies, with those marked I desire scored for the orchestra. I will have the first act of a new play finished soon. We will rehearse it while I work on the second. We can get the play out in a fortnight."

Among the books picked up at the little Italian's was "The Collegians," an intensely Irish story, with an intensely Irish heroine, written by one of the most intensely Irish of Ireland's gifted sons, Gerald Griffin. After absorbing it, Boucicault evolved "The Colleen Bawn," and, touching his mother-earth, our dramatic Antæus again won a new triumph.

This story of the evolution of the play,[1] as nar-

---

[1] Far more credible and trustworthy is Mrs. Barney Williams's version of the genesis of the play, as I had it from her own lips, and recorded by me in the "New York Dramatic Mirror," February, 1896:

"My husband [Barney Williams] and Mr. Boucicault had entered into an agreement in the fall of 1859, whereby Mr. Boucicault was to furnish us with a new Irish play to be ready in the fall of 1860. The Boucicault trademark meant a great deal in those days and carried a star a long way. Well, in January or February we met Mr. Boucicault, who read us the first two acts. The play was 'The Colleen Bawn.' My husband was delighted with the character of *Myles,* and although *Eily O'Connor* seemed a bit too sentimental for my line of business, we were both very much pleased with the play as a whole. At that time Mr. Boucicault was house dramatist for Laura Keene. Along in March he put on a play called 'Vanity Fair,' which was expected to last through the season. But it failed. Something had to replace it. Imagine our indignation and surprise to find that 'The Colleen Bawn,' which he had written for us according to contract, had been brought out at Laura Keene's! He was profuse in apologies. He had been caught in a corner, so he said, and having nothing else up his sleeve, had to give them 'The Colleen Bawn.' He would write us another piece. But my husband said, 'No.' Mr. Boucicault had broken faith with us, and we did n't propose to give him another chance. There was a little bitter feeling, but when we came to think it over we agreed that we might have done the same thing if we had had the same temptation. We are all of us human, and Dion Boucicault was very human."

This, in my opinion, is the safer story of the origin of the play, and may be adopted.

rated with great relish by Boucicault, may appear very trivial; but as one object of this book is to tell something of the wizard-like powers of the play-wright, an anecdote of this sort is perhaps needed to give an idea of Boucicault's splendid genius for theatrical necromancy.[1]

"I despoil genius to make the mob worship it," was his grandiloquent answer to the charge of plagiarism.

"The Colleen Bawn" proved conclusively that nothing can be better for an Irish dramatist than to write Irish dramas.

The Milesians, who hailed its coming with rapture at Laura Keene's Theatre on March 29, 1860, recognized in its poetry, its humor, and its raciness the first really worthy Irish play known to the stage.[2] The modest Dion came blushing before the

[1] Herman Merivale, author of "Forget-me-not" and many other successful plays, thus declared himself:

"Once let a man spin some wire-drawn story out of his own head, and he is called 'original,' no matter how stagey his characters or how stale his treatment. Dion Boucicault, a head and shoulders taller than all the rest, is denied that credit for 'The Colleen Bawn,' because he had the eye to see and the hand to fashion the materials for an old story into as original a play as ever was written. Compare the *Myles* of the story with the *Myles* of the play, and see! On the same principle, a painter who produces an 'Annunciation' should be called an adapter; and another who imagines for himself some impossible and ghastly picture, an 'original' painter."

[2] Subjoined is a copy of the announcement bill that preceded the production. I wish to call attention to the reverent way in which Boucicault confesses to the source

curtain to bow his gratitude, and if they had crowned him with a wreath of shamrocks, put the Harp of Tara into his trembling hands, and hailed him as the Shakespeare of Erin, he would scarcely have shrunk from the honors. "The Collegians" had warmly furnished forth the baked meats of the banquet; but "The Colleen Bawn" deserved its

of his inspiration. This gives the lie direct to his detractors, who said that he always ignored Gerald Griffin. Here is the bill verbatim:

LAURA KEENE'S THEATRE

A New Play By

DION BOUCICAULT

Ireland, so rich in scenery, so full of romance and the warm touch of nature, has never until now been opened by the dramatist. Irish dramas have hitherto been exaggerated farces, representing low life or scenes of abject servitude and suffering. Such is not a true picture of Irish society.

THE COLLEEN BAWN

Founded on a true history
First told by an Irishman
and now
Dramatized by an Irishman.

—

THE COLLEEN BAWN

or

The

BRIDES OF GARRYOWEN

triumph, for it is racy of the soil in which it grew, and a flower to be remembered for its fragrance and freshness.[1]

A drama by

DION BOUCICAULT

and dedicated by him to
the undying memory
of his illustrious countryman

GERALD GRIFFIN

whose beautiful romance "The Collegians" furnished the subject of the play.

Myles-na-Coppaleen	DION BOUCICAULT.
Hardress Cregan	H. F. DALY.
Danny Mann	CHARLES WHEATLEIGH.
Kyrle Daly	CHARLES FISHER.
Father Tom	DAN LEESON.
Mr. Corrigan	J. G. BURNETT.
Hyland Creagh	MILNES LEVICK.
Eily O'Connor	AGNES ROBERTSON.
Anne Chute	LAURA KEENE.
Mrs. Cregan	MME. PONISI.
Sheelah	MARY WELLS.

[1] By comparing the novel with the play, we form a higher estimate of Boucicault's genius. Although inspired by Gerald Griffin, it showed considerable freedom of invention and a large fund of originality. There are only two passages in the play which are directly taken from Gerald Griffin. One is the scene where *Danny Mann* tempts *Hardress Cregan* to put *Eily* "out of the way." The other is *Mrs. Cregan's* magnificent outburst of rant when the soldiers find her son hiding in her bedroom: "Dark bloodhounds, have you found him? May the eye that first detected him be darkened in its socket, and the tongue that told you be withered to its roots!" "The Collegians," by Gerald Griffin, may be compared with "The Colleen Bawn" as a helpful study for young dramatic authors. But those who profess to be students of the

A word about the book itself. It is now little read. But in its own day it created a sensation, the more so as it was founded on fact. Eily O'Connor was the real name of a young girl in humble circumstances. She was the daughter of a ropemaker who lived in Garryowen, then as now a suburb of the city of Limerick. Scanlan, a young gentleman of family and fortune, had married her secretly. Eventually he tired of her, and sought the hand of a lady of fortune—Miss Chute of Castle Chute. Determined to rid himself of Eily, he employed his hunchback servant, Stephen Sullivan, to take her out boating on the river Shannon and drown her. But Sullivan's heart failed him. Then Scanlan himself got into the boat. This time she was thrown into the water, one hand grasping the boat-rail, the fingers of which were promptly chopped off by a hatchet in the hands of Sullivan. Before many days her body was washed ashore on the opposite bank of the river near Kilrush in the County Clare and identified. The coroner's inquest brought in a verdict of murder against both men.

For a while no one seemed disposed to arrest so well born and highly connected a man as Scanlan. He not only walked about at liberty, but ap-

drama seldom give themselves such trouble. How many so-called Shakespearian students have gone to the Italian novelists, from whose trivial works Shakespeare is supposed to have derived some of his plots, to ascertain how far he is indebted to them?

peared at the hunt unmolested. Finally Lord
Monteagle wrote to the Castle, urging that the
scandal should be put an end to.

"You are a magistrate," came the answer from
Dublin; "the scandal is not more ours than yours.
You should enforce your own warrant."

"I felt the truth of this," said Lord Monteagle,
"and acted accordingly."

The trial of Scanlan took place at the Limerick
assizes on March 14, 1820. He was convicted, and
the date of execution fixed for March 16. He
might have obtained a reprieve even then, but a
bitter denunciation of the crime by Daniel O'Con-
nell shamed the Castle into action.

Public indignation ran so high that on the day
of the execution no conveyance could be procured
to convey Scanlan from the prison to "Gallows
Green." At last two turf-carts belonging to ten-
ants on his estate were seen approaching. The
horses were immediately taken from the carts and
attached to a carriage. But at the foot of a
near-by bridge the horses suddenly stopped, and
neither whip nor kicks nor the bayonet thrusts of
the soldiers could move them. Scanlan had to get
out and walk, amid the execrations of the multitude, who thought the action of the dumb animals
a manifestation of the abhorrence of Heaven at
the crime. He walked to the gallows between files
of soldiers, and was hanged protesting his inno-
cence to the last.

This was the story which Gerald Griffin treated

with sombre strength.[1]   He softened many of the
incidents ; he made the crime an almost involuntary
one.   It was in the delineation of the sufferings
and struggles of a weak but kindly, refined and
accomplished man who wakes up to find himself a
murderer, that Griffin's power lies.

Boucicault softens the incidents still further.   In
his play, indeed, there is only attempted murder,
unknown to and unsought by the hero.   The girl
is rescued from drowning by *Myles-na-Coppaleen,*
and in due course she is reconciled to her lover.
Strange to say, this "happy ending," thanks to the
skill of the playwright, seems both touching and
convincing.

On July 16, Mr. and Mrs. Boucicault bade *au
revoir* to New York.   Taking the play to London,
they appeared in their original rôles at the Adelphi, September 10.   "The Colleen Bawn" became
the sensation of the day, and did not outwear its
welcome for two years.   It ran three hundred and
sixty consecutive nights in London and the British
provinces, a record up to that time quite unsur-
passed in English play annals.

It has frequently been asserted that Falconer's
Irish play "Peep o' Day" anticipated "The Colleen
Bawn" as the first of the long line of romantic

---

[1] As is well known, Boucicault was not the first to find
dramatic possibilities in Gerald Griffin's romance.   Soon
after it was published, T. Egerton Wilks made a dramatization called "Eily O'Connor," which was brought out
at the New City of London Theatre, Grub (now Milton)
Street, with Ellen Tree as *Eily.*   It was an ordinary hack
version, compiled with paste and scissors.

Irish dramas.   Facts are facts.   The creator of this genre was neither Falconer nor Boucicault, but Samuel Lover, whose "Rory O'More" did so much to enhance the fame of the lamented Tyrone Power.   "Rory O'More" was the first stage romance of Ireland.   Falconer was an actor in "The Colleen Bawn," and his play "Peep o' Day" did not see the footlights until "The Colleen Bawn" had scored a record of exactly two hundred and ninety-six nights.

Queen Victoria visited the Adelphi three times during the run, and her last visit to the Boucicaults in "The Colleen Bawn" signalized her last attendance at a play-house.

"Dion Boucicault was, without exception, the most fascinating man I ever met," is the ardent confession embalmed in "Leaves from a Life." The gifted authoress was a daughter of Frith, the artist.

"Even as a child he fascinated me.   I don't know what it might have been had I been grown up. He was also extremely good-looking, and one of the most amusing talkers possible; and as he had children of his own, he used to play with them, us, and the little Fechters in a way that would have won the heart of any child.   He had married an exquisite girl called Agnes Robertson, and oh! how pretty she was!   She had the most beautiful blue eyes with black lashes, quantities of lovely black hair, and spoke with the sweetest voice possible.   She wore a red cloak in 'The Colleen Bawn,' and for some time these cloaks were greatly in the fashion.

"How simple were the Boucicaults, and the Fechters, and the delightful Sotherns in those days, and for years after, too, and how we loved going the rounds of the theatres at which they were to be seen! It is sad to think how unhappily most of the bright spirits of the theatres in the sixties ended their days. The Fechters are all dead; they quarreled and parted before the end came; the Boucicaults fell apart, too, as did the Sotherns. There seems to be something about the stage that does not make for domestic bliss; but in the days we knew them they were the happiest of people, and we were all happy together. Let us hope that somewhere the old delightful days may be found again, and all misunderstandings and miseries be wiped out.

"We never knew as much of the actresses as we did of the actors, and I fancy their time was more taken up with domestic duties than it is now, for Mrs. Boucicault rarely, if ever, dined at our house on Sundays: she worked most frightfully hard, was one of the sweetest actresses of the time, and we used generally to see her and the children in the afternoon, before the early meal which preceded the theatre. In the same way we used to see the Fechters, who were living close to them."

The "sensation" scene, showing the water-cave and the rescue of *Eily* by *Myles* after he had plunged in head first, was an eye-opener to the audiences of 1860. Transparent stage "water" had never before been seen, and a few yards of light blue gauze did more than all the fine acting of Boucicault and his wife could accomplish. By the way, these innovations—the gauze waters and the idea of *Myles* taking the "header"—were not Boucicault's. They were suggested to him by the stage carpenter at Laura Keene's Theatre the first day he was constructing the scene.

"Why not try a dive for something new?" he proposed to Dion. "A dive would go better than an ordinary jump, sir."

Boucicault saw the value of the suggestion, and lost no time in carrying it into effect. When the play was produced in Paris at the Ambigu-Comique,[1] some French carpenter or machinist further improved upon the mechanism of the "water-cave" scene. By means of a system of mirrors ingeniously arranged below a trap, *Eily* appeared to sink slowly to the bottom, and could be seen floating there until her rescue by *Myles*. One night the machinery failed in some way to work properly, and the actress, Mlle. Jeanne Essler, was so much injured that she had to keep her room for six weeks.

Boucicault has often been accused of borrowing

[1] One day in Paris, while browsing at an old book-stall on the Seine, I came upon the rarest of finds, "Le Lac de Glenaston," the French version of "The Colleen Bawn." The title-page reads as follows: "Le Lac de Glenaston, imité de l'Anglais de M. Dion Boucicault par M. Adolphe D'Ennery. Representé pour la première fois à Paris sur le Théâtre de l'Ambigu-Comique le 17 Octobre 1861."

from the French. Here was an instance where the French took from him. To Adolphe D'Ennery, that masterful *dramaturge,* was entrusted the task of decanting the Irish spirits into a French bottle; but in the process the lees were shaken up, the fine flavor lost, and the *poteen* became *vin ordinaire—* very *ordinaire.*

Crossing the Irish Channel after the London run of the play, Boucicault returned to the land of his birth and gave his country-folk a chance to admire the beauties of "the national drama." He and his wife made their first joint appearance at the old Theatre Royal, Hawkins Street, Dublin, on Easter Monday, April 1, 1861. They faced crowded houses for twenty-four nights. Had they chosen to remain longer, they would have continued to attract for many more. It goes without saying that Dion's compatriots greeted him with a hearty "Caed Mille Failthe."

A modern performance of "The Colleen Bawn" conveys little more than a tradition to this generation. To-day the play seems archaic; but a peculiar fragrance—the real smell of the peat—still haunts it. An occasional revival stirs the pulses of old-timers and astonishes the young generation, who affect to sneer at its artificial dialogue and melodramaic situations. There is no denying its perennial vitality. In this respect it towers transcendent over the puerile Irish melodramas that are manufactured afresh each season out of the effete materials of Boucicault. As Mr. Alan Dale in the "New York American" knowingly expressed it: "The Irish plays of the present day are so delightfully ephemeral that they will never go down to posterity. If they did, our grandchildren might be pardoned for wondering if their ancestors had suffered from paresis."

CHAPTER IX

Boucicault's ambitions as a manager — Converts Astley's Circus building into the Westminster Theatre — Christmas pantomime of the Grimaldi type — Fiasco of the Westminster Theatre — Boucicault's second appearance in the bankruptcy court — Provincial production of " The Poor of New York," localized for various cities — Astounding success of the play in London — Its condemnation by Charles Dickens, and Boucicault's own opinion of its trashiness.

MANAGERS of theatres who became associated with Boucicault soon learned one thing: he always endeavored to obtain the absolute direction of affairs. This disposition manifested itself during the run of "The Colleen Bawn" at the Adelphi, and led to some disputes between him and Benjamin Webster, which were finally settled by the publication of advertisements in the papers stating that while Mr. Boucicault would control the stage, Mr. Webster would direct the front of the house, which was then for the first time dubbed "auditorium." Incompatibility of temper at last caused a separation between them. Boucicault thereupon transferred himself and his play to Drury Lane Theatre.

He was then at the apogee of his fame. The profits of "The Colleen Bawn" (reckoned by some at half a million dollars, though this figure was probably an exaggeration) burned in his pocket. The restless schemes that fomented in his busy brain were craving for expansion. Nothing would satisfy him but to control a play-house of his own. The romantic idea of converting Astley's old circus building into an elegant theatre such as London had never known obsessed him.

On October 2, 1862, a letter was published in the "Times," over the signature "Dion Boucicault," advocating improvements in theatre-building, and contrasting the working expenses, the dinginess, ill ventilation and general discomfort of the London theatres of that time with the Winter Garden Theatre in New York, which Mr. Boucicault had held in 1859. In this letter he offered to head a subscription with £5000 for the purpose of erecting a suitable and comfortable London theatre.

Following hard upon this proclamation came the news that Boucicault had taken over Astley's old circus, in the Westminster Bridge Road, an establishment hitherto devoted exclusively to the exploits of equestrians, jugglers, acrobats and wirewalkers. To the task of metamorphosing this temple of the sawdust and tanbark, Boucicault now applied his best energies; and such confidence did he evince in his own power to do this, and so optimistic was he as to the outcome of the project, that he succeeded in forming a joint-stock company composed of "City men" and men of rank.

Appended hereto is a copy of the prospectus he issued:

"New Theatre Company, Limited.

"Capital, £125,000, in 5000 shares of £25 each, with power to increase. Deposit on application, £1 per share; and on allotment, £2 per share. It is anticipated that not more than £12 will be required to be called up. Two months interval between each call.

"*Patrons:* The Duke of Wellington; the Duke of Leinster; the Marquis of Donegal; the Marquis of Normanby; Earl Grosvenor; the Earl of Malmesbury; the Earl of Hardwicke; the Earl of Sefton; the Earl of Dudley; Sir John Shelley, M.P.; etc., etc.

"*Directors:* H. C. Cobbold, Esq., New Bridge Street, Blackfriars; J. W. Cusack, Esq., 12 Lancaster Gate; E. Edwards, Esq., Adelphi Chambers; Lieutenant Colonel Napier Stuart, M.P., Portman Square; Gerard de Witte, Esq., the Greenways, Leamington.

"*Bankers:* Ransom & Co., Pall Mall.
"*Auditors:* Quilter, Ball & Co.
"*Broker:* J. B. Richards, Austin Friars.
"*Offices:* 9, Cornhill.
"Secretary: H. J. Montague."

The conditions and anticipated profits of this speculation were carefully considered and calcu-

lated—so Edward Stirling[1] tells us in rather a
jocose vein. "Dividends at ten per cent. during
the building of the theatre might reasonably be
expected when the theatre opened. Mr. Boucicault's services to manage the enterprise were secured for one-third of the net profits. Although a
large number of shares were privately subscribed
for, the ignorant public held aloof, slow to believe
or accept this very promising undertaking. Fancy
twenty per cent. and a life privilege of walking in
a beautiful garden theatre, ornamented by grottos,
cascades, and endless attractions (on paper)! The
whole thing fell flat; City men did not believe in
it; West-enders simply laughed at this flight of
Dion's fancy. The idea of converting into a paradise a slough of despond, in one of the worst
neighbourhoods, surrounded by shabby, tumble-
down, ramshackle houses, inhabited by the poorest
class of petty tradesmen and waterside labourers!
Presto! by the wand or silvery tongue of Wizard
Boucicault, all these difficulties were to vanish,
giving place to a reality outrivalling the Hes-
perides of old!"

A beautiful theatre he certainly did conjure into
being. He turned the old "ring" where Astley
had disported himself into an elaborate arrangement of stalls and pit; the bygone Adelphi system
of intermediate "pit stalls" he also restored. Between the stalls proper and the orchestra was a
sort of miniature garden of shrubs, flowers and

1 *Vide* "Old Drury Lane."

fountains, the effect of which was declared to be "extremely pleasant." Another attractive adjunct was an open-air restaurant commanding a view of the river, *à la* American roof-garden, planned for use in hot weather. Alack for this Utopian scheme, with all its myriad of novelties!—it did not survive till the summer months.

Rechristened "Theatre Royal, Westminster," this temple of Dion's Muse opened its doors to the public December 22, 1862. There was a bill of prodigal richness. First came Tom Taylor's excellent little comedy "To Parents and Guardians," in which Agnes Robertson played the mischievous school-boy *Bob Nettles,* and Boucicault distinguished himself as the old Frenchman, *Tourbillon.* Then followed "The Relief of Lucknow"—or "Jessie Brown," as it was known at Wallack's, New York. Last, but not least, came an "Ideal Pastoral Pantomime," as the play-bill expressed it, entitled "Lady-bird; or, Harlequin Lord Dundreary." This was a laudable attempt to revive real English pantomime—not spectacle submerged in music-hall jests and songs, but true pantomime, in which not a word is spoken, and the meaning is conveyed by facial expression, by gesture and attitude. In the United States this delicate art, requiring skill, inspiration and patient training, enjoyed great vogue under the Ravels.[1] In Lon-

---

[1] Boucicault once startled a dinner party of literati by declaring that pantomime was the most important subdivision of the drama, and that Gabriel Ravel stood on a higher artistic plane than Charles Mathews.

don pantomime was fast losing its original significance and becoming a mere vehicle for music-hall
artists and scene-painters; it was no longer recognized as an art.   Harlequin was on his last legs;
Clown, a feeble reflex of what he was in Joey
Grimaldi's day.

Boucicault reasoned that a pantomime at Christ-
mas-time ought to be something better than a mere
spectacle full of empty glitter, with magnificently
attired figurantes and a minimum of Clown and
Columbine.

Accordingly he devised "Lady-bird," abounding
in novel incidents and fresh comicalities, but all
carried on in dumb show, in strict adherence to the
canons of the pantomime.   Even the opening, or
introduction, in which the story was told, reverted
to the old style, consisting of action only, except
in the case of the fairies, who were permitted to
explain themselves in dialogue.

It is no discredit to Boucicault's judgment to
record the grim fiasco of his pantomime.   Either
the Londoners had outlived all fondness for the
"silent fun" of the Grimaldi school, or had been
weaned away by the meretricious splendors of the
so-called pantomimes of Drury Lane and Covent
Garden.   "The utter futility of any attempt at
honorable retrogression," said a writer in "The
Gentleman's Magazine" of December, 1886, "was
amply shown by the reception given to Dion Boucicault's 'Ideal Pastoral Pantomime,' represented
almost entirely in dumb shew.   This hazardous
experiment evoked abundant enthusiasm from

critics with long memories, but the public unfortunately did not enter into the spirit of their gratifications."[1]   On Monday, January 26, 1863, the pantomime was supplanted by "The Trial of Effie Deans," dramatized from Scott, which had already been acted in New York at Laura Keene's Theatre.   An important incident worth chronicling in connection with the production was the first appearance on the professional stage of Henry J. Montague.   The subsequent career of this brilliant actor and true gentleman has been often enough related, but his early association with Boucicault, who virtually "discovered" him, remains to be told.

His father, a clergyman of the Established Church of England, had a living in Cheshire, and there Montague, whose true name was Henry John Mann, was born in January, 1843.   As he died in August, 1878, he did not live to reach thirty-six years.   His father wanted him to take clerical orders, but the lad did not care to become a clergyman and entered a banking house in London. Boucicault chanced to see him play in some private theatricals and advised him to go on the stage. While waiting to find him an opportunity to make his début, he appointed him secretary to the Westminster Theatre Company.   Subsequently, under the name of H. J. Montague, he appeared in "The Trial of Effie Deans."   He was then

[1] Huline was the Clown.

twenty years of age, and handsome as Apollo.
When he came to America, Boucicault proved a
staunch friend. He arrived in New York in 1874
to try his luck, but had secured no engagement in
advance. Boucicault introduced him to Lester
Wallack and wrote the part of *Captain Molyneux*
in "The Shaughraun" especially for him. Montague's forte was the portrayal of gentlemen;
and he was gentlemanly off the stage as well as on.
Men idolized him, and Wallack's Theatre used to
be crowded on matinée days by women who came
to see Montague act and nobody else. There was
a story current about a New York girl who turned
her closet into a shrine and burned candles around
his picture. This sounds like a press agent's fable,
but press agents were unknown at that epoch.
Whether the story was true or not, it never turned
his head. Montague was one of the founders and
organizers of the Lambs' Club of New York,
where his name is to-day cherished in loving
memory.

After the collapse of the "Theatre Royal, Westminster," Boucicault had "a grand smash." His
palace at Brompton was sold, he went through the
bankruptcy court, and London became a generally
uncomfortable place to live in. But he still felt
strong and masterful. He never said: "I 'm done
—I 'm beaten." What he did say—his actual optimistic way of putting it—was: "Successes live and
you record them. Failures are still-born children

that don't count."[1]   So, carrying with nonchalance
the ill-fortune that beset him, he kicked the dust of
the metropolis from his shoes and set out with his
better half for the provinces.   They made direct
for Liverpool.   Two managers were running a
hard and bitter rivalry in the great seaport on the
Mersey.   Alexander Henderson conducted the
Prince of Wales's Theatre, where with farce and
burlesque he made considerable money.   The other
manager, Copeland, ran the Amphitheatre with
melodrama and legitimate works.

Boucicault dug out of his trunk the manuscript
of "The Poor of New York" (even then in print
and consequently common property), localized it,
and offered it to Henderson.   That gentleman said
"he liked it well enough" and was much tickled
by a disparaging and sarcastic allusion in its text
to his rival, Copeland.   But still it did not suit the
policy of his house, where musical and frivolous
entertainment reigned, and "The Poor of Liverpool" was rejected.   Boucicault then took it to
Copeland, who thought it would suit his theatre
and put it into rehearsal.   Boucicault had completely forgotten the sarcastic allusion in the text,
and Copeland had possibly overlooked it.   When
the play was read to the company a good deal of
amusement and no small sensation arose.   The
stage manager did the reading, and in the Wil-

[1] "He left London," says John Hollingshead, "with many
debts upon his shoulders, which some little time after,
although not being bound to do so, he honorably dis-
charged."

liamson Square scene, which was equivalent to the
Union Square scene in the New York version,
Badger was made to point to the Amphitheatre—
Copeland's own theatre—and say: "Enterprise of
any kind never enters that house."

Boucicault rushed to cut out the line, which he
had written to tickle Henderson's ears, but Copeland, with whimsical perversity, ordered "no
change to be made in the text"; and during the
twelve months' run of the play in Liverpool and
its subsequent revivals there the sarcasm stood, to
the mystification of the actors and the bewilder-
ment of the public. Old Copeland used to chuckle
over the fact that he had found Boucicault's measure in two different lines.

At all events, "The Poor of Liverpool" accomplished its author's purpose: put money in his
purse and was voted a great success. The "house
on fire," with the realistic conflagration, falling
shutters, etc., the arrival of the real engine and
horses, and the thrilling escape of *Badger* from the
blazing ruins, created a genuine sensation.

Encouraged by this success in Liverpool, Boucicault turned again to the metropolis and offered his
wares to various managers. He declined to accept
five or ten pounds a night as a royalty for the performance of the play; he boldly demanded a share
of the profits. The London managers resisted
what they termed an unprecedented demand. The
indefatigable author replied: "I can wait till one
of you finds himself in a tight place." He had
not long to wait. George Vining, manager of the

Princess's Theatre, was close on the verge of ruin. Boucicault stepped in. "What are your expenses?" he asked. He was told they were seventy pounds a night. He offered to allow the first hundred pounds taken nightly to be appropriated by the manager, thus giving the theatre thirty pounds a night clear profit, and after that whatever was left should be divided. Vining hesitated, and talked the scheme over with other managers, who exerted all their influence to break down the negotiation. Boucicault then promptly offered to secure Vining by paying down ten thousand pounds and taking the receipts, whatever they might be, during the first hundred nights. Vining was so astounded at such a proposal that he closed with the first offer. The opposition of the associated managers was defeated; "The Streets of London" was produced August 5, 1864; and the Princess's Theatre became one of the successful and popular houses.

A letter from Charles Dickens to John Forster is the best informant on the success of the play. "I went the other night," wrote Dickens, "to see 'The Streets of London' at the Princess's—a piece that is really drawing all the town, and filling the house with nightly overflows. It is the most depressing instance, without exception, of an utterly degrading and debasing theatrical taste that has ever come under my notice. For not only do the audiences—of all classes—go, but they are unquestionably delighted."

That Boucicault himself set no value upon the

play[1] save as a money-making product, and that his opinion of its intrinsic worth coincided with that of Dickens, the following letter, written at about the same time, amply testifies:

ROYAL HOTEL, GLASGOW,
March 13.

DEAR STIRLING:

"When the wind blows, then the mill goes"; and Fortune's gale is making my mill spin round like blazes. I have developed a new vein in the theatrical mine, and one in which you can have an interest beyond that you always feel in my success.

I have tried the bold step of producing—originally in the provinces—a sensation drama, without aid or assistance of any kind. The experiment has succeeded.

I introduced "The Poor of Liverpool"—a bobtail piece—with local scenery, and Mr. Cowper in the principal part. I share after thirty pounds a night, and I am making a hundred pounds a week on the —— thing.

I localize it for each town, and hit the public between the eyes; so they see nothing but fire.[2] *Et voilà!*

[1] The original, it may be remarked, was a five-act French drama entitled "Les Pauvres de Paris," by MM. E. Brisbane and Eugène Nus, first acted in 1856 at the Ambigu-Comique.
[2] The sensation scene was a burning house.

I can spin out these rough-and-tumble dramas as a hen lays eggs. It's a degrading occupation, but more money has been made out of guano than out of poetry.

Believe me, very sincerely yours,

DION BOUCICAULT.

Harry J. Montague as *Captain Molyneux* and Ada Dyas
as *Claire Ffolliott* in "The Shaughraun"

CHAPTER X

Boucicault in his native city — Peculiar relations existing between him and John Brougham — First production of "Arrah-na-Pogue" in Dublin — Social success of the Boucicaults in the Irish capital — "Arrah-na-Pogue" rewritten and produced in London — Translated into French and acted in Paris — Boucicault's new version of " The Wearing of the Green," the Irish national anthem.

THE charges of plagiarism that followed Boucicault around the world did not weigh heavily upon his conscience. He claimed the right to choose the material that suited him, and his art lay in fashioning it into fresh forms and imbuing it with new meaning and beauty.

"Genial John" Brougham is credited with saying: "Och, sure, Dion is the boy for borrowing and stealing. His first experience in passing off the works of others was at the age of four years, when he wrote the whole of 'Paradise Lost' in a neat and distinguishable hand, and presented it to his mother as his own composition."

Whereupon Boucicault was moved to remark gravely: "Originality, speaking by the card, is a quality that never existed. An author cannot exist without progenitors, any more than a child can. We are born of each other."

There was something paradoxical in the per-

sonal relations existing between Brougham and
Boucicault.   Face to face, they were affectionate
compatriots, brimful of mutual admiration.   What
they said of each other behind each other's back
was "a horse of another color," their remarks
ranging all the way from indulgent sarcasm to
bitter vindictiveness.   Mr. William Winter has explained this anomalous situation by quoting Dr.
Johnson's sage remark: "Sir, the Irish are a fair
people.   They never speak well of one another."

The autumn of 1864 found the "Genial John"
and the dapper Dion in their native city in the land
of the shamrock.   Long an exile from Ireland,
Brougham, as actor, author and manager, had
written his name large in the annals of the American stage.   At the outbreak of the Civil War he
had left New York and joined forces in London
with Charles Fechter, whom he furnished with one
of his most effective plays—"The Duke's Motto";
and now, at the urgent pleading of Boucicault, he
came to Dublin to originate the rôle of *Colonel
Bagenal O'Grady* in a new Irish play, "Arrah-na-
Pogue," fresh from Dion's pen.

Of all the characters Boucicault drew, he said he
considered the jovial, urbane Irish gentleman
O'Grady the best as a true type—because the most
unconscious.   Brougham, after hearing him read
the play, agreed with him in this opinion, adding
with true *O'Grady* unconsciousness: "He is a great
part, but where are you going to get a man to play
him?"

Brougham had forgotten that the part was written to fit himself.

He was the living embodiment of *The O'Grady,* and this portrait of the gay and gallant Hibernian afterwards took rank with his *Sir Lucius O'Trigger* in the esteem of his admirers. Boucicault has left it on record how, night after night, he used to stand unseen in the prompt entrance to drink in Brougham's exudation of the magnanimous Celtic spirit in his realization of *The O'Grady.*

It was highly apposite that the city which gave Dion Boucicault birth should see the first production of one of his best and most characteristic plays; and not only that, but in a more truly Irish form than any audience saw again. "Arrah-na-Pogue" had its first production on any stage at the old Theatre Royal, Hawkins Street, on November 7, 1864. Well mounted with new scenery by F. Lloyd, it had an excellent cast. Besides John Brougham as *The O'Grady,* Boucicault and his wife appeared as *Shaun the Post* and *Arrah Meelish;* William Rignold as *Beamish M'Coul;* Mrs. Buckingham White as *Fanny Power;* Jack Reynolds as *Michael Feeney;* and Sam Emery (the father of Winifred Emery) as the uncanny *Grannya.*[1] The verdict was more than favorable; crowds filled the theatre; and the play, though much too long, aroused hearty enthusiasm.

[1] This character of a half-crazed hag, whose son had suffered death by the rope in the "Rising," made a deep appeal to the Dublin audience. It was afterwards eliminated as being a mere incidental figure and unnecessary to the development of the story.

On the 25th of November it was performed by command of the Lord Lieutenant and Lady Wodehouse, the curtain on that night rising at 8.30 o'clock. After this endorsement of "the Castle," Boucicault became the lion of the hour in his native city. People pointed him out to one another in promenading Sackville Street or driving through Stephen's Green. The grand folk of Merrion Square showered social invitations upon him. His own debonair ways and his wife's charm of manner made them welcome in Dublin drawing-rooms for their own sakes, quite apart from the interest attaching to them as stage favorites. They were frequent guests at the house of Sir William Wilde (Oscar's father), and at Lady Ferguson's, wife of Ferguson, the poet.

"Once in Dublin," relates Mr. Percy Fitzgerald, "I was invited to a party given on a rather eccentric principle. It was to commence with a lunch at two; there was a concert, conversation, and tea to follow, until dinner was reached. This was, as may be imagined, a serious original business, for there were a large number of persons to be provided for. After the dinner there was a dance. The hostess was Mrs. Parnell, mother of the uncrowned King—an agreeable American lady with handsome daughters. It was here that I met Dion Boucicault, who was at the height of his reputation. He was an interesting, and even brilliant man, and greatly followed by the public gaze, for he was assumed to be safe and clever, shrewd and far-seeing. With him was his charming wife, the original attractive *Colleen Bawn* of the scarlet cloak. They were a happy and affectionate pair, and she seemed to have great pride in her husband's gifts. How in this case, as in so many others, came a disastrous change, is well known. In his dramatic work Boucicault had a firm, unerring touch. He was a most accomplished playwright.

"At this time he was on the point of bringing out, at the old Theatre Royal, Dublin, his second Irish drama, "Arrah-na-Pogue," and it was extraordinary what pains he took, and what sagacity he showed, in the preparation. I was present at the first performance. It was an altogether different piece from what it afterwards became. There was a last act, in which there was an Irish duel, in a room where the faithful *Shaun* is so carried away by his excitement as to stand before his master, regardless of the opponent's pistol which 'covered' him, and eagerly direct his aim. Meeting him on the next day, and congratulating him, he entered gravely on a discussion of the subject. To my surprise, he quietly pointed out that the last act would never do and must come out altogether. The rest must be rewritten, the interest concentrated. He was glad that he had made the experiment, as it gave him the opportunity of removing sad defects. This was an instructive lesson in the craft. Accordingly, when it was reproduced in London, I could scarcely recognize it."

John Brougham played in both versions,[1] and when he heard that the first piece was undergoing revision he remarked that he could not conceive what the author wanted more than the success the play had obtained in Dublin. Everything had gone swimmingly—even the Lord Lieutenant had come in state to see the production. Just then the curtain went down on one of the acts, and the two went out before it to take the call. *Sotto voce* to Boucicault, amidst the hail of cheers, Brougham said: "Damn it, Dion, what do you want better than that? Can't you leave well enough alone?"

But Dion was not to be deceived by the exuberant enthusiasm of an emotional Irish audience. After the Dublin run ended on December 17, he set to work to rewrite the play. It is instructive to trace the same hand working out two distinct forms from the same material, as a sculptor while shaping a *chef d'œuvre* makes several groups before he finally concludes on the best. The last act was entirely new. In it was introduced the mechanical effect of *Shaun's* escape from his cell in the old tower, followed by the climb up the ivied wall and the rescue of *Arrah* from the clutches of *Feeney*. This was looked upon as a triumph of illusion.

Boucicault scheduled the new version for production in London at the Princess's Theatre on

---

[1] One of the best speeches in the play, that uttered by *O'Grady* on going off in the second act, "Oh, Father Adam, why did n't you die with all your ribs in your body?" was Brougham's own interpolation.

March 22, 1865. A month or six weeks before
that date he read the play to the assembled actors
in the greenroom, and John Brougham listened
attentively to the revisal. After the reading he
went up to Boucicault and, taking him affectionately by the arm, said: "Now I understand the
secret of your success. It is in the indomitable
perseverance and the fastidiousness that induce
you to better your own work at any cost or any
amount of labor. This is a much better play than
the other."

All of which goes to prove the truth of one of
Boucicault's pet aphorisms: "Plays are not written; they are rewritten."

"Arrah-na-Pogue" enjoyed the most substan-
tial sort of a success in London. Applauded to
the echo by English audiences, it established a
sort of *entente cordiale* between John Bull and
Paddy.

France next paid homage to Boucicault. A
better fate awaited "Arrah-na-Pogue" in Paris
than had been meted out to "The Colleen Bawn."
Faithfully and adequately translated into French
by M. Eugène Nus, who gave it the title of "Jean
la Poste; ou les Noces Irlandaises," the play ran
for one hundred and forty nights at the Gaieté; and
at a subsequent revival at the Porte Saint Martin,
in 1876, again delighted the Parisians.[1] Boucicault must have chuckled with self-satisfaction to
find another of his Irish plays an exportable

[1] "Jean la Poste," discussed by Zola in "Le Naturalisme
au Théâtre," pp. 404-7.

product. The long run of "Arrah-na-Pogue" in the French capital discountenanced the prevalent belief among London managers that their successes were incapable of transference to Paris. Furthermore, it gave the lie to Boucicault's detractors, who declared that every play from his pen had a French origin.

But by far the most noteworthy feature in connection with "Arrah-na-Pogue" was the new birth in this play of the old street-ballad, "The Wearing of the Green."[1] The original song appears to date back to about the year 1798. At the suggestion of his mother, who remembered some

[1] When Boucicault first sang the song in London on the opening night of "Arrah-na-Pogue," there was a storm of protest. The blowing up of Clerkenwall prison by the Fenians was an event of recent occurrence. Against the advice of his manager and friends, who implored him not to sing it, he persisted. Then came an edict from the cabinet ministers of Queen Victoria prohibiting the singing of the song in Great Britain; and for years, although it thrilled the heart of every Irishman, it was never heard in the British dominions.

Had Boucicault lived till the Queen paid her last visit to Ireland, when she consented to the wearing of the shamrock, he would have beheld, as the royal party landed from Her Majesty's yacht, the dragoons, fusiliers and lancers drawn up in full uniform to salute their sovereign, a sprig of shamrock on every breast, and the Queen greeted by the song she had once forbade—"The Wearing of the Green."

In the intervening years, said an eye-witness on this occasion, the melody that seems to hold all the pathos of Ireland had been sung from the cabins of Connaught to the camps of Irish regiments fighting England's battles from the Cape to Afghanistan. Kipling has told, in "Namgay Doola," how it had reached to the mountains of Thibet.

of the lines, Boucicault unearthed the old melody,
wrote new words and introduced the song in the
wedding scene at the end of the first act of the
play. "The Wearing of the Green" has been described by a writer in the London "Athenæum"
as probably the finest street-ballad ever written;
it deserves to be called the Irish National Anthem
—if any piece of poetry can claim that title; it
has become the standard song of Irish patriotism.
The bands play it and prima donnas sing it. It is
heard oftener than any of Tom Moore's ballads,
and its popularity is constantly growing.

CHAPTER XI

Home life of the Boucicaults in London — Joseph Jefferson arrives from Australia — First production of "Rip Van Winkle"—Just how far Jefferson is indebted to Boucicault for his imperishable creation.

I DO not wish to overload my pages with quotation, but a certain latitude in this matter is allowable and indeed necessary. John Hollingshead, in his autobiography, "My Lifetime," gives the following perfect pen picture:

"The Boucicaults lived close to their work (1865), in the upper part of a house in Regent Street, nearly opposite the old Polytechnic, surrounded by a large and young family,[1] happy themselves, and a source of happiness to many others—myself amongst the number. Boucicault was a patient and constant worker—a

[1] Three of Boucicault's children, by right of heritage, have gained distinction behind the footlights. Miss Nina Boucicault has acted charmingly in a wide variety of parts on both sides of the Atlantic. Mr. D. G.—who used to be known as 'Dot' in America, but has now taken his father's name—worthily perpetuates that name, and is esteemed the most expert stage manager in London to-day. Aubrey Boucicault's brilliant personations of *King Charles II* in "Mistress Nell," and *Karl Heinrich* in "Old Heidelberg," are readily recalled. The untimely death of Aubrey on July 10, 1913, occurred in the New York Hospital. All three Boucicaults showed themselves possessed not only of talent, but of facile versatility. That gift seems to run in the Boucicault blood.

temperate man, simple in his habits, who treated
dramatic authorship as a trade. He worked
harder than a banker's clerk, and made his
brother, who acted as his secretary, work also.
Early and late, he never idled, and after his pleasant little dinner parties and social gatherings he
regained his lost time by increased industry. For
a year or more I had daily and hourly opportunities of witnessing this happy life, and the making
of at least one great theatrical reputation. Joseph
Jefferson, an unassuming actor from America—
gifted, as he afterwards proved, with the most
pathetic humour—dropped into the little circle
one day with an idea, to be blessed in a few weeks
with 'Rip Van Winkle.' In due course he appeared at the Adelphi with Boucicault's piece, and
under Boucicault's unrivalled stage management,
and made himself the admiration of England and
America. His impersonation of Washington
Irving's immortal dreamer was never seen without arousing a feeling of affection for the actor."

"Rip Van Winkle" was produced at the
Adelphi Theatre on September 4, 1865, and ran
for one hundred and seventy nights.[1] Mrs. Billington played *Gretchen,* and Paul Bedford and

[1] The first "Rip" play dates back almost to the time of
the publication of Washington Irving's story in 1819. The
exact date and place of production are unknown. As
early as May 26, 1828, a version entitled "Rip Van
Winkle; or, The Spirits of the Catskill Mountains" was
acted at Albany, New York, with Thomas Flynn in the
title part. Charles B. Parsons, James H. Hackett and
Charles Burke were among the earliest actors of *Rip.*

Felix Rogers were in the cast. Christopher J. Smith, the pantomimist, enacted the silent dwarf with the keg. The "business" arranged by him for Mr. Jefferson was always afterward followed by those who played this part.

The idea of the spirits of Hendrick Hudson and his crew remaining silent was the happy inspiration of Jefferson. It was the actor's delicacy of art in his treatment of the scenes in the mountains that made the Catskill spooks at all convincing. In all the old versions of "Rip," they talked and sang. "Rip Van Winkle" proved Jefferson's *pièce de résistance* for the rest of his long and successful career, and will doubtless prove his passport to the consideration of posterity.[1] That the success of Boucicault's version of "Rip" was due almost solely to Jefferson's acting, I do most potently believe. That Washington Irving's scant little story was an unactable proposition till Boucicault touched it with his wizard's wand, is proven by history. Here is Boucicault's story of the genesis of Jefferson's success:

"He walked into my study in London, and I rose

Charles Burke, half-brother of Jefferson, appeared in his own version at the Arch Street Theatre, Philadelphia, in 1849, supported by Jefferson as *Seth,* the innkeeper. In later years Jefferson and Hackett both used this version, although the first version produced by Hackett had been made by Bayle Bernard as early as 1832.

[1] "It was Dion Boucicault," says Clement Scott, discussing the evolution of the play, "who placed the pinnacle on a solid foundation and crowned the work built up stone by stone."

with sincere pleasure to greet my old colleague, Jefferson. This was in 1865, and in summer-time. I had not seen him for five years. Who remembers the Winter Garden where he played *Caleb Plummer* in 'Dot' and *Salem Scudder* in 'The Octoroon' in 1859? During these intervening years he had been westwards in Australia; I had been in London.

"Jefferson was anxious to appear in London. All his pieces had been played there. The managers would not give him an appearance unless he could offer them a new play. He had played a piece called 'Rip Van Winkle,' but when submitted to their perusal they rejected it. Still he was so desirous of playing *Rip* that I took down Washington Irving's story and read it over. It was hopelessly undramatic. 'Joe,' I said, 'this old sot is not a pleasant figure. He lacks romance. I dare say you made a fine sketch of the old beast, but there is no interest in him. He may be picturesque, but he is not dramatic. I would prefer to start him in a play as a young scamp—thoughtless, gay, just such a curly-headed, good-humored fellow as all the village girls would love, and the children and dogs would run after.'

"Jefferson threw up his hands in despair. It was totally opposed to his artistic preconception. But I insisted, and he reluctantly conceded.

"Well, I wrote the play as he plays it now. It was not much of a literary production, and it was with some apology that it was handed to him. He read it, and when he met me I said: 'It 's a poor thing, Joe.' 'Well,' he replied, 'it is good enough for me.' It was produced. Three or four weeks afterward he called on me, and his first words were: 'You were right about making *Rip* a young man. Now I could not conceive and play him in any other shape.'

"How small a thing is a seed, yet how grand a tree springs from an acorn! Irving supplied the seed without which the dramatist would have been barren, and Jefferson would have possibly remained a statue without a pedestal—prostrate, unrecognized and unknown."

This anecdote, which, by the way, has become a part of stage history, is not intended to prove the play of "Rip Van Winkle" a great and glorious masterpiece. On the contrary, it is the veriest potboiler, and without Joseph Jefferson would not have long endured. But without Boucicault's clever turn of the wrist, the subtlest of actors could never have made the rôle of *Rip* attractive.

As *Rip Van Winkle,* Joseph Jefferson burst into world-wide fame and his name became a household word among English-speaking people.

The which is writ in dramatic history!

CHAPTER XII

Boucicault's industry and fecundity for nine years —
Melodramas galore — Charles Dickens at rehearsals
of " The Long Strike" — Henry Irving's first hit.

THE barest mention must now suffice of
Boucicault's works during the next nine
years. Actors on both sides of the Atlantic profited
by these plays; reputations and fortunes were
made by the array of characters they furnished to
the stage. But the field here grows too wide to be
dealt with in detail.

"The Parish Clerk," written for Joseph Jefferson (May, 1866, at Manchester, England), provided that rare actor with a lovable, sympathetic
rôle upon which he lavished all the resources of
his delicate art. The play proved fundamentally
weak, however, and was forthwith shelved.[1] At
the Lyceum Theatre, September 15, 1866, Charles
Fechter produced Boucicault's domestic drama,
"The Long Strike," suggested by Mrs. Gaskell's
stories "Mary Barton" and "Lizzie Leigh."
Charles Dickens, who was on terms of closest in-
timacy with Fechter, took sufficient interest in the
production to "assist" at rehearsals, as he tells us
in a letter to Forster. Possibly Boucicault may

[1] Derived from "Le Maître d'Ecole," one of Frédéric
Lemaître's last rôles. Boucicault had seen him in it, and
conceived the idea of reshaping it for Jefferson.

have availed himself of some suggestions from the great novelist. The cast was a strong one, including the author as *Johnny Reilly*, a sailor; Mrs. Boucicault as *Jane Learoyd;* Sam Emery as *Noah Learoyd;* J. C. Cowper, a Liverpool favorite, as *Jem Starkie,* and H. Widdicombe as *Moneypenny.* Simultaneously with the London production, the play was given in New York at the Olympic Theatre. J. H. Stoddart scored an overwhelming hit as *Moneypenny,* the irascible old lawyer whose brusque and churlish exterior hides a kind and tender heart. "The Long Strike" was an admirably effective play, and the telegraph scene exemplifies Boucicault's stagecraft at its best.

In the same year, on Saturday, October 6, on the occasion of the opening of the Holborn Theatre, "The Flying Scud" was first seen. It was one of the first of that interminable series of plays called "racing dramas," full of direct claptrap appeals which the gallery never fails to answer. "The Flying Scud" flew away with high stakes, both in London and in New York (Wallack's, April 24, 1867). But the critics shook their heads in sorrow and said that Dion Boucicault was called to higher things.

November 5, 1866, saw "Hunted Down; or, The Two Lives of Mary Leigh" at St. James's Theatre, under the management of Louisa Herbert. This play owes its origin to a French drama, "Femme à Deux Maris." It was the happy instrument in bringing Henry Irving to the front. Originally produced at the Princess's Theatre, Manchester, in the previous August, Kate Terry played *Mary Leigh* and Henry Irving was the *Rawdon Scudamore*. Ever alert to scent latent genius, Boucicault was keenly alive to the unusual power displayed by Irving. Accordingly he stipulated with Miss Herbert that when "Hunted Down" was acted in London, she should engage the then unknown actor. His judgment again proved unerring, and Irving made a strong impression as the down-at-heel gambler who bullies his patient, broken-spirited wife with relentless cruelty.

Charles Dickens, on seeing Henry Irving in "Hunted Down," said enthusiastically: "Mark my words, that man will be a great actor." [1]

On Monday, April 29, 1867, E. A. Sothern was seen in a play called "A Wild Goose Chase" at the Haymarket. This was a dramatization by Boucicault of "Lady Leigh's Widowhood," a military novel that had appeared in "Blackwood's Magazine" and hit the popular taste of the day. Lester Wallack derived his "Rosedale" from the same source. No such success attended "A Wild Goose Chase," which was a long, rambling affair. Sothern appeared as *Captain Robert Devlin,* and had the support of such fine players as Henry Howe, Buckstone, Caroline Hill, Ione Burke and Mrs. Chippendale.

At the Prince of Wales's Theatre, "How She Loved Him" was produced on December 21, 1867 (it had been tentatively acted at Wallack's, New

[1] This has been verified by the novelist's son, Mr. Henry Dickens.

York, in May, 1865). The Bancrofts built high hopes on its success in London. H. J. Montague played *Dick Heartley,* and Marie Wilton, *Atalanta Cruiser.* Sir Squire Bancroft, who made a hit as *Beecher Sprawley,* says in his memoirs that all went well up to the end of the third act, when a situation went all wrong, and the rest of the play was not allowed to redeem the mistake. He appears to have regretted it, as the piece had genuine merit. Boucicault called it a comedy of character and conversation.

This failure was soon forgotten in the controversy excited by "Foul Play," in which he collaborated with Charles Reade.[1] It was produced at the Holborn, May 28, 1868. Charles Reade grew very wrathy when a critic exposed its French origin, "Le Portefeuille Rouge," by MM. Fournier and Meyer.

Reade stoutly maintained that he knew nothing of the French play, and brought suit for libel against the journal that accused him of plagiarism. "Foul Play" has been wantonly travestied

[1] "This collaboration gratified Charles Reade more thoroughly than any during his lifetime; and although he could chaff Mr. Boucicault as a 'sly fox,' esteemed both his society and his friendship very highly. On one occasion, when a remark was hazarded in disparagement of a drama by this gentleman, he turned contemptuously on the speaker with the query: 'Will you find me another man in England who could write such a play?' Nor was his belief in Mr. Boucicault ever shaken—indeed, he envied his capacity for commanding both the tears and laughter, the astonishment and delight of the gallery."— *Memoirs of Charles Reade,* by Charles L. Reade and the Rev. Compton Reade, 1887.

by F. C. Burnand in an astounding work—"Chik-kin Hazard, by Charles Readit and Dion Bouncey-core."

"After Dark: a Tale of London Life" had a rousing success at the Princess's Theatre, August 12, 1868. Boucicault probably drew his inspiration from "Les Bohémiens de Paris" by MM. D'En-nery and Grangé (Ambigu-Comique, September, 1843). An earlier version, called "The Scamps of London," was the work of W. T. Moncrieff, au-thor of the celebrated piece "Tom and Jerry." Heretofore Boucicault had been content with a single sensation scene to one melodrama. "After Dark" had half a dozen. Realistic reproductions of familiar localities in London: the underground railway, with the startling rescue of a drugged man lying on the tracks; the arches of London Bridge, where the vagrants "roosted"; a music-hall in full swing—these were some of the alluring attractions of "After Dark." The public taste was tickled. An abundance of excitement for their money suited the patrons of melodrama exactly. Their purveyor never pretended that he was pro-viding art or literature, but he supplied a com-modity with a good marketable value. He simply catered to the multitude; and where the multitude gathers, there do dividends grow. The heart of Mr. Vining, manager of the Princess's Theatre, re-joiced and was exceeding glad, and another in-stance was given of Boucicault's acuteness in pandering to the public.

During the run of "After Dark" he was at-

tacked with nervous prostration, which obliged
him to retire to private life. But the ruling passion would not be bidden, and in the seclusion of
his retreat he adapted "Presumptive Evidence"
from "Le Courrier de Lyons." This followed
"After Dark's" nine months' run at the Princess's
on May 10, 1869. It was in two acts, a much
shorter play than Charles Reade's accepted version,
"The Lyons Mail." Mme. Celeste appeared as
Josephine Dubosc.

"Formosa; or, The Railroad to Ruin" was another "thriller," produced at Drury Lane on August 5, 1869. The Oxford-Cambridge boat-race
constituted the chief feature of the play. The title
"Formosa" was derived from the name of an
island in the China Sea—Formosa, "the most
beautiful." Another feature was the alleged portrayal of the inner life of a questionable class of
feminine society—the demi-monde. Thus arose a
"tempest in a teapot" between the press, which de-
nounced the play as immoral, and the management
of Drury Lane. This, of course, helped to swell
the profits. Chatterton, the manager, and Boucicault are said to have cleared more than twelve
thousand pounds between them. Shakespeare—
poor bard!—had been playing in the same theatre
to empty benches. "Formosa" retrieved the fallen
fortunes of Drury Lane.[1]

---

[1] It was Boucicault, of course, who craftily stimulated
the attacks of the press, knowing full well that they would
excite the public curiosity to see so "immoral" a play. In
a letter to the "Times" he originated the oft-quoted

It is worth noting, by the way, that Henry Irving again emerged into prominence by his intense acting of the dastardly villain, *Compton Kerr*. Katherine Rogers was *Formosa,* "the most beautiful." When the play was first given in New York at Niblo's, September, 1869, Ada Harland made a captivating *Tom Eden,* and Charles R. Thorne was the *Tom Burroughs.*

"Lost at Sea," which opened the season at the Adelphi, October 2, 1869, was another lurid melodrama, the joint work of Boucicault and Henry J. Byron.

Two more adaptations from the French—"Paul Lafarge," with W. Rignold in the title rôle, and "A Dark Night's Work," derived from Scribe, with Rose Leclercq as the heroine—comprised the bill at the Princess's Theatre, Monday, March 7, 1870.

"The Rapparee; or, The Treaty of Limerick" was a romantic Irish drama with a vague sort of historical background, produced on September 2, 1870. Sheil Barry made his first London appearance in a comedy part, the *Doctor,* in this play.

On December 5 of the same year, at the Holborn Theatre, "Jezabel; or, The Dead Reckoning," founded on "Le Pendu" by MM. Michel Masson and Anicet Bourgeois, fell far short of expectation.

"Elfie; or, The Cherry Tree Inn," a domestic drama with a mysterious murder episode, received a trial production at the Alexandria, Liverpool,

aphorism, "Shakespeare spells ruin, and Byron bankruptcy." The letter appeared over Chatterton's signature, but was really written by Boucicault.

Monday, May 1, 1871, and was acted at the Gaiety Theatre, London, the following November. William Rignold, a sound and natural actor who had originated rôles in several of Boucicault's plays, enacted *Joe Chirrup,* a blind sailor. Twenty years afterward he was stricken with real blindness.

"Kerry" (also called "Night and Morning") was an adaptation of the charming *lever de rideau,* "La Joie Fait Peur," and first saw the footlights at the Gaiety, London, November 29, 1871. *Kerry,* the old Irish majordomo, so inimitably enacted by the author, again proved Boucicault to be a master in the art of lifelike portraiture. His characterization was everywhere pronounced a gem without a flaw, perfectly conceived and executed with consummate mastery. It was in the part of *Kerry,* I may add, that Boucicault made his last stage appearance.

CHAPTER XIII

Partnership with the Earl of Londesborough — They lease Covent Garden — A fortune squandered on "Babil and Bijou" — Return to America — Boucicault's fine acting in "Daddy O'Dowd" — Writes a play for John McCullough about the American Civil War.

IN 1872, Boucicault, in partnership with the Earl of Londesborough, leased the Covent Garden Theatre, where, on the night of August 29, the curtain rose on the magnificent fairy spectacle, "Babil and Bijou." About eleven thousand pounds, it was roughly estimated, was squandered on the production. Asked by Lord Londesborough, a munificent patron of the drama, to write a play or comedy, Boucicault conceived the idea of a colossal spectacle which should eclipse anything ever before attempted within the four walls of a theatre. He called upon his old friend, J. R. Planché, famed for his charming extravaganzas and fairy pieces, and together they collaborated on "Babil and Bijou."

At rehearsals poor old Planché was almost wholly ignored, Boucicault cutting and slashing the long rhymed speeches which his friend had laboriously evolved. Planché consoled himself with a famous witticism. To an abnormally tall young lady who had a leading part and who asked him to write her a song, he responded: "My dear, Longfellow is your man."

Hervé, then little known, composed the music, and Rivière superintended the choruses, among which was "Spring, Spring, Beautiful Spring," written for boys' voices and sung by choristers with splendid effect.

An army of men, women and children took part. There were dancers, comedians, pantomimists, Amazonian warriors and coryphees galore, together with a huge fantastic aquarium of pseudo oysters, crabs, cockles, seals, periwinkles, sea-lions, sea-horses, sharks, alligators, sword-fish, devil-fish and lobsters—scarlet boiled lobsters at that!—at the bottom of the ocean (possibly it was the Red Sea).

The action transpired in every conceivable realm, from mid-air to the bowels of the earth. The principal parts were filled by Joseph Maas, the tenor, Lal Brough, Mrs. Howard Paul, Mrs. Billington and Annie Sinclair. The *première danseuse* was Mlle. Henriette Dor, a graceful exponent of the classic school of ballet.

But the most conspicuous figure on the overcrowded stage was a stately damozel of remarkable beauty, Miss Helen Barry, who made her début in this piece as the *Princess Fortinbras*. Gasps of ecstatic "Ahs!" filled the big theatre when she swept down to the footlights, leading the Amazonian march.

Boucicault has been generally censured for mak-

ing ducks and drakes of his patron's money, as
well as for his abrupt and mysterious retreat to
America immediately following the first performance. But it must not be overlooked that he
had worked hard, early and late, for the success of
the venture, and had expended an enormous
amount of futile labor upon details. A nervous
breakdown was the inevitable consequence. "Babil and Bijou" was successfully revived at the Al-
hambra in 1882 and had a long run.

Again taking up his abode in New York, Boucicault at once set to work turning "La Tentation"
of Octave Feuillet into English and called it "Led
Astray." Admirably acted by artists like Charles
R. Thorne, Stuart Robson and Rose Eytinge, it
filled the coffers of the Union Square Theatre
(December 5, 1873). Boucicault claimed a creator's percentage for his work and was paid it. In
June, 1874, "Led Astray" was acted in London
at the Gaiety with Charles R. Thorne and Robson,
who were imported to play their original rôles. It
is said that Boucicault mailed a cheque for fifty
pounds to M. Feuillet just before the London production, not because he was legally bound to share
royalties with the Frenchman, but simply as a tribute to M. Feuillet for "inspiring" him.

"Mora; or, The Golden Fetters," acted at Wallack's, New York, May, 1873, did not have even
the merit of providing the actors with effective
occupation, a quality seldom lacking in Boucicault's plays.

"Daddy O'Dowd," first seen at Booth's Theatre,

March 17, 1873, had for its basis a French domestic drama of great heart interest, "Les Crochets du Père Martin," by MM. Cormon and Grangé. The same work had provided the story of "The Porter's Knot," with which Robson as *Sampson Burr* used to electrify his audiences. Boucicault, in transferring the scene to Ireland, gave the play new atmosphere, and his own performance of the old Galway fisherman was the most moving and affecting thing he ever did on the stage. It was simple pathos, but none the less poignant. "Daddy O'Dowd" was afterward acted in Dublin and London, and while there was but one opinion concerning Boucicault's acting,—the best he had ever shown in any play,—the drama never gained vogue.

"Mimi" was first acted at Wallack's in July, 1873. It was a free adaptation of "La Vie de Bohème" by MM. Henri Murger and Théodore Barrière. Boucicault himself had the heroic part of *Maurice Durosel,* and Katherine Rogers that of *Mimi.*

The season at Booth's Theatre opened on August 10, 1874, with a new play, "Belle Lamar," founded on incidents in the American Civil War of 1861–65. John McCullough, Katherine Rogers and Frederick Warde[1] sustained the leading rôles. There was a fine effect at the rise of the curtain: the singing of the sentinel on a summer night on the banks of the Potomac. "Belle Lamar" con-

[1] His first appearance in the United States.

tained many stirring and effective incidents, and deserved to succeed, but it did not. For four weeks it held the boards, thanks to extravagant advertising and the indiscriminate "papering" of the house. It was then withdrawn, and a new version, by Boucicault, of Otway's "Venice Preserved" produced on September 14, with John McCullough as *Pierre*. A notable feature of Boucicault's version, says Mr. William Winter, was the introduction of the famous curse scene from the last act of Byron's "Marino Faliero," a passage upon which, in some sapient quarters, the adapter was warmly congratulated.

CHAPTER XIV

*First production of "The Shaughraun"—An apprecia-
tion by George William Curtis—The blackguards in
Boucicault's Irish plays—A school of Irish actors
comes into existence—"The Shaughraun" in London
—A modest letter to Disraeli—Row with Chatterton
at Drury Lane—Fatal accident to Boucicault's eldest
boy, Willie.*

THE treasury of Wallack's Theatre was in a
depleted state when Boucicault walked in
with the manuscript of "The Shaughraun" and
turned the ebb of disaster into the full flood of
prosperity. Produced on November 14, 1874,[1] the
play changed the luck of the theatre in one night,
and Wallack's coffers overflowed for months after-

[1] *Captain Molyneux* . . . . . H. J. MONTAGUE.
Robert Ffolliott . . . . . J. B. POLK.
Father Dolan . . . . . . JOHN GILBERT.
Corry Kinchela . . . . . EDWARD ARNOTT.
Harvey Duff . . . . . . HARRY BECKET.
Conn the Shaughraun . . . . DION BOUCICAULT.
Sergeant Jones . . . . . MR. LEONARD.
Mangan . . . . MR. JOSEPHS.
Reilly . . . . E. M. HOLLAND.
Sullivan . . . . C. E. EDWIN.
Doyle . . . . MR. PECK.
Arte O'Neale . . . . . . JEFFREYS LEWIS.
Claire Ffolliott . . . . . ADA DYAS.
Mrs. O'Kelly . . . . . . MME. PONISI.
Moya . . . . IONE BURKE.
Bridget Madigan . . . . . MRS. SEFTON.
Nancy Malone . . . . . MISS BLAISDELL.

wards. The actual receipts for Thanksgiving Day matinée alone were $2,550.50, the highest figures registered in a New York box-office up to that date.

Once again Boucicault struck the national note, and his transplanted countrymen found a new thrill of enthusiasm in welcoming *Conn the Shaughraun,* "the life of every fair, the soul of every funeral, and the first fiddle at all the weddings and patterns in the parish." The play was the product of Boucicault's long apprenticeship to the stage. It was wrought with a full knowledge and ripe experience of all the tricks of technique, and with the perfect craftsmanship of an expert playwright. Critics called it a "mosaic" of things pieced together from here, there and everywhere. So, indeed, it was. But it had a freshness, a spontaneity, an inspiration all its own. It breathed out free animal spirits, Hibernicism of thought and feeling; and its Lever-like scenes had a vigorous and vital nationality. It was a remarkable achievement for a man who had been so many years before the public, during which time he had poured out a constant stream of plays, good, bad and indifferent. 1841–1874! From "London Assurance" to "The Shaughraun"! What years of hardy endeavor lay between those two dates! What an expenditure of brain and energy!

Yet at the age of fifty-five or thereabout, the playwright burst with all the effulgence of youth upon the public, and Boucicault went back to eighteen when he stepped on the stage as *Conn O'Kelly.*

Made up in his ragged red coat, with his kit slung across his broad back, with his curly brown hair and ruddy cheeks, he looked the roguish boy to the life. His voice had the cheery ring of youth, his smile had lost none of its brightness, his art none of its cunning. When he spoke of his faithful companion, "Tatthers," a dog never seen but much talked of in the play, the animal seemed a tangible reality. To one who had preserved the graces of a youthful style of acting through so long service behind the footlights and so many vicissitudes of fortune, *Conn the Shaughraun* seemed to give a new lease of life. And this in spite of the fact that the physical exigencies of the part were by no means slight.

After his first entrance and he had spiritedly described the glories of the "hunt in full cry," when he borrowed *Squire Foley's* horse and "the baste ran away with his characther," Boucicault was perforce obliged to jump in and out of cabin windows, to scale prison walls that revolved in full view of the audience apparently without human agency (would that all Irish prisons were constructed on this plan!), to climb over abbey ruins and execute a "back fall" down a precipitous "run"; after being "stretched out" and "waked" as a genuine corpse, to come to life for a hand-to-hand encounter with a pair of ruffians; and finally, from the inside of a barrel, shoot through the bung-hole at the arch villain *Corry Kinchela*, and afterward place the barrel over the colleen *Moya*, thereby concealing her

from view.[1] These and numerous other exploits
of *Conn* might have taxed the physical resources
of a younger man than Boucicault, but the veteran
romped through the play like a two-year-old colt,
with unquenchable gusto.

While "The Shaughraun" was in rehearsal, Wallack rose at the title. Who on earth would be able
to pronounce such a name, and who but a Gaelic
antiquarian could tell the meaning of the mystify-
ing word? But Boucicault was adamant before
the pleadings of Wallack and the company. "The
Shaughraun" it must be, and "The Shaughraun"
it was.

As a matter of fact, Boucicault coined the word,
or, to speak precisely, he corrupted a Gaelic par-
ticiple into a noun. In the language of the Gael, *to
go a-shaughraun* means to go wandering or to go
tramping. By converting the word into a substan-
tive, Boucicault used "shaughraun" in the sense of
"vagabond"; wherefore "Conn the Shaughraun,"
Anglicè, became "Conn the Vagabond."

Indulging his foible for romantic anecdote,
Boucicault was wont to relate a fictitious yarn
about the haphazard way in which the costume of
Conn was evolved. On the first night of "The
Shaughraun" he arrived at the theatre two hours
before the curtain went up, and was met by his
dresser, who asked him what he was going to wear

[1] This last incident of the barrel was taken in its en-
tirety from "Long Tom Coffin," a Surrey piece, wherein
T. P. Cooke, the famous actor of sailor parts, executed
the same "business" more than half a century before.

for the part of *Conn*. The question reminded him
that he had been so busy with other people that he
had forgotten to provide for himself. They
mounted into the wardrobe of the theatre.

"Have you got an old red hunting-coat? Where
is your *Tony Lumpkin* dress? Surely you have a
Goldfinch coat?"

"But, sir, they will not fit."

"That is just what I want. Tear the arms to
make them shorter; slit up the back—so. What
have you there? *Tony Lumpkin's* hunting-cap—
black velvet—the very thing! Tear the lining out.
I see a splendid pair of old boots yonder."

"Those are not a pair, sir."

"So much the better."

And thus in half an hour the costume of *Conn*
was patched together. What an escape!

Much likelier was it that Boucicault went early
to the wardrobe room after a careful study of a
volume of Lever's "Jack Hinton," containing the
inimitable illustrations by "Phiz." One has only to
look at the pictures of *Tipperary Joe*[1] by "Phiz"

[1] *Tipperary Joe* is perhaps the most memorable character in "Jack Hinton." Lever's last introduction to the
novel tells us that *Tipperary Joe* was a real personage:
"Those who remember the old coaching days between
Dublin and Kilkenny will recall the curious figure, clad
in a scarlet hunting-coat and black velvet cap, who used,
between Carlow and the 'Royal Oak,' to emerge from
some field beside the road, and after a trot of a mile or
so beside the horses, crawl up at the back of the coach
and over the roof, collecting what he called his rent from
the passengers; a very humble tribute, generally, but the
occasion for a good deal of jesting, not diminished if an

Dion Boucicault as *Shaun the Post* and Sadie Martinot
as *Arrah* in "Arrah-na-Pogue"

to see where Boucicault got the inspiration for
Conn's costume.

It was always one of Boucicault's noted charac-
teristics that many of the best things in his plays
were suggested to him at rehearsal. His alert
mind would catch a hint from any accident. Then
the clear, sharp, authoritative ring of his "Stop!"
would, like the rap of the conductor's baton, bring
everybody "upstanding." In rehearsing a play, he
was likened to a French cricket on an Irish griddle.
"Wait a moment," he would say. "We'll have
that scene over again, Mr. Montague. I've some
new business."

It was a very rich ham, was "The Shaughraun,"
after he had stuck it full of these cloves. And how
he built up Harry Montague as *Captain Molyneux*
by shouting "Stop!" and then firing a new piece of
business at him!

He flashed bits of humor and cunning devices of
action at rehearsal, threw in telling lines and
groupings, and so built up the picture and the
episodes. His fecund brain had been doing this so
long that it came to the finishing touches with an
automatic facility.[1]

English traveller were present who could neither com-
prehend the relations between *Joe* and the gentlemen, nor
the marvellous freedom with which this poor ragged fellow discussed the passengers and their opinions."

[1] Mr. Daniel Frohman told me the following anecdote
showing how Boucicault studied his audiences and ex-
tracted the full value from a "situation." In the scene at St.
Bridget's Abbey by moonlight, he brought the curtain
down on the two gunshots denoting the escape of *Robert
Ffolliott* to the lugger waiting to transport him across the

A most sympathetic appreciation of the play, as it was acted at Wallack's, appeared in "Harper's Magazine" for July, 1875. It came from the pen of George William Curtis, than whom we have never had a more delightful dramatic essayist since Charles Lamb. I quote *in extenso:*

"There has been no play since 'Rip Van Winkle' which has excited so much interest as this, and no character which is a more distinct figure in the mind than the *Shaughraun*. He is an Irish good-for-nothing, a young vagabond who is as idle as *Rip Van Winkle* and who loves the bottle—not to *Rip's* excess—and who by his nimble wit and laughing, careless courage serves to good purpose a pair of very amiable lovers. There are knaves and wretches in the play, and ladies and lovers, and soldiers, and a priest and old crones. There is some kind of a story, as there is in an opera, but you don't remember very well what it is. It is only a background for the *Shaughraun* to sparkle on. Some grave critic remarked that as a play it had faults; it violated canons and laws, and wanted unity, and did many things which it seems plays ought not to do. There are two plots, or threads, or catastrophes, and the mind, it appears, is distracted, and the whole thing could have been much

Atlantic. But the curtain fell in cold silence. So he wrote in an anticlimax with explanatory lines, literally hammering into the heads of the audience the significance of the gunshots. Hey, presto! The curtain thereupon descended upon deafening applause. Verily, as Dion himself was wont to say, playmaking is a trade like carpentering.

better. Ah! had the painter only taken more pains! But, on the other hand, Mr. Critic, there is not a dull word or a dragging scene in it. It moves from beginning to end, and is pure picture and romance all the way. There are, indeed, those dreadful moral difficulties which we have been called upon to consider in 'Rip Van Winkle.' Here is a lazy good-for-nothing, who has no trade or profession, or even employment, who has been in jail for his tricks more than once, who carries a bottle in his pocket, and poaches and fishes at his will, and he carries with him our admiration and sympathy, and puts our mind into any mood but that of severity and reproof. He is simple and generous and sincere, and brave and faithful and affectionate, indeed, but he is a mere *Shaughraun,* after all.

"Perhaps the only plea that can be urged in the defence is that the play leaves us more kindly and gentle. But if you return to the charge and ask whether this might not have been done had the hero been a respectable and virtuous young man, keeping regular hours and reputable society, avoiding strong liquors and vagabondage, and devoted to an honest trade or a learned profession, the Easy Chair can only ask in return whether *Hamlet* might not have been a greengrocer. The charms of 'The Shaughraun' are those of 'Rip Van Winkle'— they are its humanizing character and influence. Here is the spectacle of knavery brought to naught, of faithful love rewarded, and all by means of simplicity, generosity, good nature, and courage. Things are very perplexing if that is

immoral. It is, in fact, a poem, a romance. The
little drama is wrought, indeed, with all the consummate skill of the most experienced and accomplished of play-writers. The resources of the stage
—machinery, surprises, whatever belongs to effect
—are all brought most adroitly into play, and the
spectator is compelled to admire the result of tact
and experience in the construction of a drama. But
it all deepens the romantic impression. The scene
is Ireland, the story is one of love, the chief actor
is an Irishman seen by the imagination; and it is
one of the felicitous touches of the skill with which
the work is done that from time to time, when the
spectator is most intent and his imagination is all
aglow, there is a faint breath from the orchestra,
a waft of wild, pathetic Irish melody which fills
the mind with vague sadness and sympathy, and
the scene with a nameless pensive charm. This is
the stroke of true humor—the mingled smile and
tear.

"But as you sit and watch and listen, you become
more and more aware that the keynote of the
whole play is very familiar, and even what the
Easy Chair has already said may suggest the essential resemblance, which gradually becomes fixed
and absolute. Under a wholly different form, under circumstances entirely changed, in another time
and country, and with a myriad divergences, the
'Shaughraun' is our old friend, 'Rip Van Winkle.'
It is recognized as readers of Browning recognize
'In a Spanish Cloister' in the dialect poetry. The
motive of the two dramas is the same—the win-

ning vagabond. In the earlier play he is more
indolent and dreamy, and the human story naturally fades into a ghostly tale; in the later he is
heroic and defined, and acts only within familiar
and human conditions. As a study of the fine art
of play-writing, you can easily fancy, as the
performance proceeds, that an accomplished playwright, pondering the great and true and permanent success of 'Rip Van Winkle,' may have set
himself to pluck out the heart of its mystery, and
to win the same golden victory upon another field.
You can fancy him sitting unsuspected in the par-
quet on Jefferson's nights, intently poring upon
that actor's impersonation of the character that he
has 'created,' studying it with a talent of infinite
resource for the object in view, and gradually re-
producing, under a wholly new and foreign form,
the fascination of a spell that is peculiar to no
country or clime, but inheres in human nature. It
is doubtless a fancy only, but it holds with singular
persistence. What is the *Shaughraun* but a jocund
Irish *Rip*, or *Rip* but a *Shaughraun* of the Cats-
kills?"[1]

On September 4, 1875, the *Shaughraun* made
his first bow to a London audience at Drury Lane,
then under the management of F. B. Chatterton.

---

[1] "The Shaughraun" had not been running long at
Wallack's before another Irish play called "The Skibbeeah" was acted further down the street at the Theatre
Comique, 514 Broadway. Tony Hart, in a character similar to *Conn,* gave a remarkable copy of Boucicault. The
two plays were so exactly alike in plot, situation and character, that Boucicault lost no time in instituting proceed-

Conn's success with the Britishers was unequivocal: he kindled the same popular enthusiasm as in New York, and the play yielded almost as rich a harvest at Drury Lane as at Wallack's. The cast, however, was inferior to the New York cast, with the single exception of Sheil Barry, who, because of natural qualifications, excelled Harry Becket in the rôle of *Harvey Duff*. This character of the traitorous police spy had its prototype in real life— a despicable cur who went among the poor people in Ireland, passing himself off as a "Fenian head-centre"; then, after learning their secrets, swearing information against them and pocketing the "blood-money." When one section of the country grew too hot to hold him, he would betake himself to another district and there renew operations as a government informer. Wherever he went, he contrived to gain the confidence of the peasantry by pretended loyalty to the Fenian movement. Woefully did he betray that confidence. Often he perjured himself, and his false oaths sent innocent men to the gallows or across the sea to

ings for an alleged infringement. The author of "The Skibbeeah" (Gaelic for "hangman") coolly put in the unique plea that both plays were stolen goods, and he submitted to the court a long list of scenes and episodes purporting to be all antecedents of "The Shaughraun." But the court did not take Mr. G. L. Stout's defence seriously and decided in favor of Boucicault, thus banishing all apocryphal "Shaughrauns" from the field.

penal servitude. Most galling of all, this pesti-
lence in human form was a born and bred Irishman.

In *Harvey Duff,* Boucicault reproduced the
venomous creature with unflinching realism, and
Harry Becket, the original representative of the
part at Wallack's, was effective enough to excite
the execrations of the Irish in the gallery. But
the *Harvey Duff* of Sheil Barry was really nothing
less than a work of genius. Irish himself, his per-
ceptions were keener, his understanding of the
character finer than Becket's. What the audience
saw was the veritable Judas Iscariot of the Irish
race, a human being at once pitiable and loathsome.
It was a stage creation recognizably true. All that
saved it from becoming absolutely repulsive was a
touch of the old ineradicable humor inherent in the
Celt.

The blackguards in Boucicault's Irish plays are
really very subtly diversified and contrasted.
*Michael Feeney, Danny Mann, Mr. Corrigan,
O'Leary* in "The Amadan," *Harvey Duff,* and the
rest of the rapscallions are individual in the highest
degree. To the graphic interpretation of these
parts came a small army of Irish actors, so strongly
sympathetic with Boucicault's creations that they
shared in his success. Dominick Murray, Falconer, Sheil Barry, W. A. Scallan (not to be con-
founded with W. J. Scanlan, the beloved singing
comedian), W. B. Cahill, "Jack" Reynolds, Joseph

A. Wilkes, Dan Maguinness, Frank Breen, and Gus Reynolds are the names that come freshest to memory in this connection.

While disporting himself as *Conn* every night, Boucicault found time to indite numberless glowing eulogiums about himself and his play, which appeared in the advertising columns of the London journals. The modern press agent was then unknown. Had that very important and influential factor in the theatre of to-day existed in Boucicault's time, he would most assuredly have learned a trick or two. Boucicault was not content with "booming" himself in the press. He found it necessary to address no less a personage than Mr. Disraeli, then Prime Minister, and, in his own name, as the author of "The Shaughraun," demand the release of all Irish political prisoners then languishing in English prisons.

Either Disraeli was unmoved by Boucicault's plausible arguments, or perhaps he was powerless to act on his own authority in the matter. Certain it is that no prisons flung open their doors; no gracious reply came from the Prime Minister by way of apology.

Undaunted by "Dizzy's" chilling disdain, Boucicault determined to derive some glory, at least, from his patriotic protest. He succeeded in getting his letter to Disraeli printed throughout Great Britain and America. Perhaps this was as much as he had ever hoped for. At any rate, it kept his

name and "The Shaughraun" for a long time in
the public eye.

Here is the letter *in toto:*

To THE RIGHT HON. B. DISRAELI.

  Sir:

    During the last five months we have been
representing before the English people in London
a play entitled "The Shaughraun." The work is
founded on an episode in the Fenian insurrection
of 1866. As a literary effort it has no pretensions,
therefore no poetic clothing disguises its subject;
it possesses no wit to divert public attention from
this simple story:

    A young Irish gentleman has been tried, con-
victed and transported to the penal colonies for
complicity with the rebellion. He escapes to America, and from thence ventures to visit his home in
Ireland. A police emissary discovers his presence,
he is rearrested, consigned to prison, from which
he escapes, and eventually is restored to freedom
by a general pardon, granted (under poetical
license) during your ministry. This pardon is the
Deus ex machina of the drama.

    I call to witness 200,000 of the people of London
who have been present at this representation during one hundred nights; I call to witness the press
that have recorded the result, to declare that I have
stated simply and without guile the scenes and incidents composing this work; and I call the whole
world to witness this spectacle—the government of

England, with a full and noble reliance on the loyalty of the English people, authorizing and approving the representation of this play, thus inviting daily a jury of two thousand citizens to hear and pronounce their feelings on a great political question.

In all countries, and at all times, since the political license of Aristophanes was reprobated by the Athenian tyrant to the present day, when the French censor watches with minute jealousy every expression of their drama, the theatre has been acknowledged a sensitive test of public opinion. Some person may hold the expression of public sympathy in a theatre to be a matter of little weight; but a little weight has turned a scale, and a feather thrown upon the surface of the sea may serve to indicate its tide or current.

It was surely not the cunning of the dramatist nor the great merit of the actors that lifted the whole audience to their feet, as cheer after cheer shook the old walls of the National Theatre when the fugitive convict escaped from his prison. Surely there is no attempt throughout the play to deceive the spectator as to the nature of the sympathy they extend; they are plainly invited to sympathize with one who is endeavoring to elude the penalty of a great offence. Why do they watch his progress with interest? and when an announcement is made that Her Majesty's pardon has been granted to all the political prisoners, why are these words greeted with hearty applause? May we answer, It is because the English people have begun to forgive the offence, and heartily desire to forget it? So I believed when I wrote this work, with the deliberate intention to ask that question in plain language, and I have done so. The question has been put nightly one hundred times to two thousand people of all classes, from the Prince and Princess of Wales to the humblest mechanic in the city, and there has been no dissentient voice upon it—no, not one! I have delayed calling your attention to this matter until the last moment, when I withdraw the play forever from the London stage. I am no politician, sir, but a working-man in that guild of literature whereof you are the most distinguished living member. If I venture out of my mental depth in approaching the subject, hold out generously your hand to one who loves his country and its people, and feels that affection to be his only eloquence. All the leaders of the Fenian outbreak are at large; a few obscure men still linger in chains, and these are, I believe, the only British citizens now in prison for a political offence. I am not capable of judging what benefit the spectacle of these sufferers may be to society, but I can see the detriment occasioned when punishment exceeding the measure of retribution makes Justice appear capricious, and tends to turn the criminal into a martyr. I have seen, and I know, that toward these twelve or fourteen miserable men are directed the sympathies of 20,000,000 of English hearts in American breasts—English hearts that sincerely respect their mother country, and would love her dearly if she would let them.

One crowning act of humanity would be worth a dozen master-strokes of policy; and the great treaty to be established with the United States is neither the Canadian fisheries nor the border-line on the Pacific Ocean—it is the hearty cohesion of the English and the American people. Those who say the time is not come for the exercise of clemency, forget that mercy is not a calculation, but a noble impulse—that no man keeps a fallen foe under his heel but a coward who dares not let him up. In reply to such objection I would answer, if the time has not come for the prudent exercise of Her Majesty's prerogative, let your noble impatience push forward the hands of the clock—its strike will be heard in millions of grateful hearts, and your own, sir, will not feel the worse either here or hereafter.

> Your very obedient servant,
> DION BOUCICAULT.

THEATRE ROYAL, DRURY LANE,
    January 1, 1876.

For some intimate details about "The Shaughraun" in London I am indebted to the late John Coleman, who, in his readable memoirs, "Actors and Playwrights I Have Known," succinctly reports an interview with F. B. Chatterton, manager of Drury Lane at this time.

"There was a capital house the first night, and on the second (Saturday) we went up to three hundred and sixty pounds.

"During our rehearsals the lady who was to play

Moya 'dried up' at the last moment.[1]   We had to induce Mrs. Boucicault to play the part, and as there were internal dissensions going on which ripened soon afterwards into an open rupture, the operation required a good deal of delicate diplomacy.

"You remember how admirably Boucicault played *Conn,* and how handsome the fellow looked. Well, one night, Falconer[2] came around to see me after the play, and while discussing some matter of business Boucicault walked into the room.

"He was denuded of his hyacinthine locks (of course you know that his head was as bald as a billiard ball), and he had an atrabilious look, as if he had just eaten something which did n't agree with him.   The rival dramatists accosted each other with more courtesy than cordiality; indeed, if they were cordial in anything, it was their dislike for each other.   The success of 'The Shaughraun' was wormwood to the author of 'Peep o' Day'; so, taking stock of Boucicault's cadaverous mug, Falconer said:

"'Ah, Dion, how well *you* look *on* the stage!'

---

[1] It was intended that Rose Cullin should play *Moya,* but at twenty-four hours' notice Mrs. Boucicault undertook the part.

[2] Edmond Falconer (real name O'Rourke) worked in rivalry with Boucicault, but fell far behind.   The protégé of an old gentleman named Falconer, who gave him access to his library, he took his patron's name when he went on the stage.   He scored a hit as the deformed *Danny* in "The Colleen Bawn," in the first London production at the Adelphi Theatre—his first and only hit,

" 'Yes,' replied the other; 'and how well *you* look *off* it!'

.   .   .   .   .   .

"For the brief space of a few weeks I enjoyed the supreme felicity of being the manager of the three most successful theatres in London. 'The Shaughraun' at Drury Lane with Boucicault, and 'Rip Van Winkle' at the Princess's with Jefferson, filled these theatres nightly. The money literally poured in, but Boucicault had his usual facility for making things pleasant.

"At the beginning of the last week he said to my acting manager: 'Saturday is my last night, and I should like a little demonstration—merely such a demonstration as an artist has a right to expect on such an occasion. I therefore request that the pit, gallery and upper circle may not be overcrowded. Issue fifty tickets less than the usual number in each part of the house, and debit me with the deficit.'

"Of course, my man immediately communicated with me on the subject. I smelled a rat, and having ascertained that the greater portion of the boxes and stalls had been taken by Boucicault's friends, I reserved the remainder for my own.

and after a row with Boucicault left the cast. He then brought out his own play, "Peep o' Day," at the Lyceum Theatre. Falconer is often credited with having preceded Boucicault as the "originator of Irish romantic drama." This is an undeserved honor. "The Colleen Bawn" had been running for over two hundred nights in London when "Peep o' Day" was produced for the first time on November 7, 1861.

"In point of fact, I anticipated a scene, a seditious speech, and an organized demonstration against the Government, to enable Dion to make his exit to America amidst a blaze of fireworks. Being forewarned, I resolved to be forearmed, and took my measures accordingly. When the curtain rose the house was crowded, the audience fervid and demonstrative. At the end of the first act, there was a double call, and a laurel wreath with green ribbons was cast at Boucicault's feet.

"At the end of the second act he was called for again and again, and pelted with shamrocks. At nine o'clock I arrived. I had barely got inside the theatre when an inspector of police came up. The man was pale and livid, and could scarcely gasp out his awful intelligence.

"There had been an accident on the Great Northern Railway, near Huntingdon, in which poor Willie, Boucicault's eldest son, had been killed. The news knocked the breath out of my body.

" 'Good God!' I exclaimed. 'How is the father to know it?'

" 'Don't trouble about that, sir,' said the inspector. 'I 'll go and tell him.' And the man was actually bolting around to the stage door to blurt out the fatal news there and then, had I not seized and muzzled him. One thing was quite certain: the tidings must be kept from Dion and his wife till they got home. So, giving imperative orders that no one was to be admitted behind the scenes, I made my way on to the stage, where, the very moment I entered, I encountered Boucicault face to face.

"He accosted me somewhat defiantly with:

" 'So you 've turned up at last.'

" 'Yes, I 've come to do honor to the occasion,' I replied.

"I had a bad time of it for the next hour, for I had to keep up a smiling face and try to talk upon indifferent subjects, thinking all the while of how the news was to be broken.

"Willie had been the apple of his father's eye. If there was one human being that Dion Boucicault loved in the world besides himself, it was that poor boy.

"At last, with the end of the play and the customary calls and recalls, came a roar from Boucicault's partizans: 'Boucicault! Speech! Speech!'

"This was responded to by a counter-roar from my myrmidons of 'No! No! Chatterton!'

"I remained in the prompt entrance, prepared for all emergencies. At last the uproar in front culminated in a tumult, during which it seemed as if the house was coming down about our ears.

"Boucicault, who had gone to his dressing-room, came down, and, meeting my stage manager, remarked in the most ingenuous manner:

" 'Dear, dear, this is dreadful! Where is Chatterton?'

" 'There,' replied the stage manager, pointing to me; whereupon Dion came up and inquired:

" 'Don't you think I 'd better go on?'

" 'No,' said I, sturdily. 'I don't think anything of the kind.'

" 'I really must,' said he.

" 'You really must n't,' said I.

" 'But they 'll tear the house down.'

" 'It 's my house, not yours, so that 's my look-out!'

" 'By G—! I will go on!' snarled Boucicault, savagely.

" 'Then you 'll have to walk over my body first, and when you 've done that my carpenters have their orders to prevent your going on. Now look here! Let 's talk common sense; you 've had your little innings; you 've had all the compliments, all the honors that any actor or author could desire, but your engagement is over. So it 's no good "kicking against the pricks." '

"With that, we glared at each other. Then there was a lull in the storm in front. After a minute's reflection he simmered down and said in his pleasantest manner:

" 'Very well. Come to my room, have a glass of wine, and let us shake hands, anyway.'

"So that difficulty was over, but 'the greatest was behind.' Dion was now at his best, and was as jolly as he could be; and when he was jolly he was one of the pleasantest fellows breathing. Mrs. Boucicault was—as she always was—charming. The difficulty was, how to tell them of their bereavement.

"I was unequal to the task, and so I left them. When I got on the stage my man told me that our family physician, Dr. R——, and Boucicault's brother William were both in front of the curtain. I went around and told them what had occurred as well as I could. We then arranged for William Boucicault to get Dion home, and the doctor kindly undertook to be in waiting at Langham Place to break the sad intelligence.

"Ill news spreads apace, and I found, on returning to the stage, Miss Foote and Mrs. Edmund Phelps crying bitterly, and waiting to descend with their condolences on the poor mother when she came out of her dressing-room; but I bundled both the ladies out of the theatre, for which, of course, I was put down as an unsympathetic brute!

"I had a cab waiting at the royal entrance in Maiden Lane, and when Mrs. Boucicault came downstairs I packed her into it, saying that Dion had gone home and wished to see her immediately. She turned pale, and looked dubiously at me.

" 'There 's nothing wrong, Mr. Chatterton— nothing about W-Willie?' she inquired.

"I had n't the heart to tell her, so I said, 'Nothing particular; only Dion has a friend or two to supper, and he wants you at once.'

"With that she drove off.

"She would know the news soon enough—too soon! Poor little woman, it was a sad thing for her—sadder for her than for any one.

"How futile and puerile seemed all our miserable quarrels in the presence of this calamity!

"God knows how the father and mother passed that night. I only know I never closed my eyes till

morning, for thinking of the poor lad who lay dead
at Huntingdon."

Dion William (Willie) Boucicault was Dion's
eldest son, born at New Orleans in 1855. The railway collision at Huntingdon, England, in which he
met his death, occurred on January 29, 1876, and
he lies buried there. The father purchased a large
plot of ground and inclosed it as a garden.
Desirous to make the town of Huntingdon itself a
monument to his son, Boucicault offered to erect,
in his name, any public building the corporation
should consider most required. (Be it noted that
Boucicault was then a man of means, thanks to the
continued prosperity of "The Shaughraun.") The
people of the town were convened to decide the
matter, and they asked that the grammar school
should be rebuilt. Boucicault raised a noble pile of
buildings on the market-place of Huntingdon,
which was finished and inaugurated on the 10th
of May, 1877, the anniversary of his boy's birth-
day.

Whereupon some Irish journals discovered that
Oliver Cromwell, having been born in Huntingdon,
was probably educated in the grammar school of
that town. They accused Boucicault of restoring
a place in which the enemy of Ireland was educated. The accusation was somewhat far-fetched.

On the spot to which the body of his son was
first taken after the catastrophe, Boucicault erected
a drinking fountain, composed of masses of red
granite, forming a lofty pile of rocks, on which is
a kneeling marble figure, life-size, of a girl drink-

ing at a pool. She holds a sea-shell to her lips. The inscription on this monument is taken from his play "The Trial of Effie Deans": "Water is truth. It cleanseth a man and bringeth up his food from the earth. It maketh of•him a Christian, and is the only earthly thing that God hath permitted to rise up and inhabit the heavenly sky."

CHAPTER XV

Enormous profits of "The Shaughraun"—Boucicault's prodigality — Last appearance of the Boucicaults together in New York—Agnes Robertson's return to England.

"THE SHAUGHRAUN" is believed to have netted its author over five hundred thousand dollars. Why, after the amazing run of this play, did he not retire to his study and give the remainder of his life to literary work, in honor and prosperity? Doubtless he scorned a life away from the theatre; he had too much of the unrest and petulant fire of youth. "Power seemed to reside in him exhaustless." At sixty he still felt invincible, and his restless nature kept him in harness. But his decline in a double sense set in when "The Shaughraun" was shelved.

It was beyond the mathematics of even those who knew best to tell what he did with the profits. His good-fellowship, his profligate generosity, his magnificent recklessness are not yet cold in the memory of those who still speak with dazed wonder, not unmingled with admiration, of the strange career and the strange endowment of this extraordinary man.

Thus was Boucicault, like Samson, careless in his days of strength!

"Fortune has perched on my banners," he once

wrote to a friend, "and I have earned very large sums of money, but have reserved very little. My family have had it, and there are so many calls on one's sympathy. Besides, I do hope that I shall die without more than enough to bury me decently. It seems to me much better to give one's property to one's heirs while you are alive and can see the enjoyment it produces. Why heap it up, to be wrangled for after you are gone? Post-mortem prudence rarely turns out rightly. Sufficient for this life are the troubles thereof! Ah, no. I don't want any one to wait for my death with greedy hopes of any benefits. Such a position of affairs hardens the hearts of those about you and turns human beings into ghouls that feed upon the dead. I wish I deserved such an epitaph as this : 'He lived like a prince and died worth a shilling, owing no man a penny, but leaving a record written in smiles and good humor. So do not shed a tear over him who never intentionally caused one to flow.' "

A fine, sunshiny philosophy this, as long as one's worldly possessions survive; but on the coming of adversity the sunshine somehow fades, and the shadows, like spiders, creep in and disconcert the philosopher.

Boucicault reached the plenitude of his powers in "The Shaughraun." The chronological record of his later work, from play to play, is not exactly enlivening.

"Forbidden Fruit" (Wallack's, 1876), one of the first and best of the errant-husband farces, owed its origin to two French pieces—"Le Procès Vauradieux" and "Les Dominos Roses." After a successful run in New York, it was produced at the Adelphi, London, July 3, 1880. Mr. G. A. Sala, who certainly knew his Paris, found great fun in telling his readers in the "Illustrated London News" how utterly unlike the life of ordinary English mortals was this eccentric picture of contemporary manners, as transplanted from Paris to London. The *cabinet particulier* in London in 1880 seemed a most amusing anachronism.

"Marriage," a comedy made over from "Le Chapeau de Paille d'Italie" (Wallack's, 1878), was preceded by some trumpet-blowing on a very large scale. Boucicault, it appeared, felt it his duty to rehabilitate dramatic literature. His public words were: "Hitherto I have given you bunting. I propose now to furnish point-lace." Whatever the material of the play may have been, its texture was not strong; it was more perishable than point-lace.

"Clarissa Harlowe," founded on Richardson's *chef-d'œuvre,* enlisted the services of Charles and Rose Coghlan (Wallack's, 1878). It aroused a languid sort of interest and then expired. Boucicault remarked in a note on the programme that he had been moved to dramatize the celebrated old novel by reason of the recent interest in the work excited in Paris by the panegyrics of M. Jules Janin. New York did not respond.

On Monday, February 10, 1879, Mrs. Boucicault—who played under her endeared name of Agnes Robertson—came forward at Booth's Theatre, where she appeared with her husband in their old rôles, in a revival of "The Colleen Bawn."

Mr. William Winter, in describing the event, said in the "Tribune": "Mr. Boucicault's desire seemed to be—as doubtless it was—that the evening should belong to his wife; that she should have a glad triumph, and should enjoy it; and that *his* work should be to augment the pleasure and emphasize the success by scattering at her feet the shamrocks and the clover of a chivalrous loyalty." A week was devoted to revivals of his Irish plays, ending on Saturday, February 15, when Mr. and Mrs. Boucicault played together for the last time on any stage. Mrs. Boucicault soon afterward returned to England.[1]

[1] The last stage appearance of Agnes Robertson in America was at the Columbia Theatre, Chicago, September, 1887, in a play by Bartley Campbell called "My Geraldine." She assumed the character of *Mary Carroll,* and her son Aubrey was also in the cast.

CHAPTER XVI

"Irishisms"—Boucicault becomes lessee of Booth's Theatre, New York—Début of his son "Dot"—Extraordinary performance of "Louis XI," with Dion as the crafty monarch—A lecture on pronunciation at the Lyceum Theatre, London, before English actors.

IN 1879 the ubiquitous Boucicault became the lessee of Booth's Theatre, New York. With two cherished objects in view, he shouldered this responsibility: one was to introduce to the public his son Darley George ("Dot"); the other was to gratify his own ambition to appear as *Louis XI*.

He engaged a company and began his tenancy of Booth's with the production of "Rescued," a conventional melodrama with the customary "sensation" scene. The piece failing to attract, he decided to play his trump-card without delay, and his own version of Casimir Delavigne's tragedy was forthwith announced. It was no mere actor's vanity that induced Boucicault to undertake *Louis XI*. He sincerely believed that he could interpret the character better than Charles Kean, Couldock, W. E. Sheridan and Henry Irving, the four great representatives of the rôle, each of whom had scored individual triumphs.[1]

---

[1] The rôle of *Louis XI* seems indeed to be susceptible of more than one conception. The extraordinary portrait which Philippe de Comines, Brantôme and other historians

As this event was one of the most extraordinary and amazing in Boucicault's variegated career, it almost deserves a special chapter. The late George Clarke, who was for me a mirror of things perished, regaled me with the story. Here it is precisely as he told it to me and as I immediately afterward jotted it down.

"I was at the time a member of Boucicault's company," said Mr. Clarke, "but had not been cast for anything in 'Louis XI.' On the night of the first performance I happened to be back on the stage, talking to some of the boys, and as I passed by the 'star dressing-room,' I noticed that the door was half open and Boucicault sat before his glass making up. He caught sight of me and called me to come in. He was nervous almost to prostration, and was slapping on the grease-paint profusely and indiscriminately.

" 'I can't seem to get this make-up right,' he said, turning full around upon me. If it had been any one but Dion Boucicault, I should have burst out laughing. He looked more like a Sioux or a Kickapoo in full war-paint than the wily French mon-

have left us of the subtle and remorseless monarch of the fifteenth century, who welded the various chieftainships of Gaul into the French monarchy, stimulated Samuel Phelps and Charles Kean to diametrically opposite conceptions. The late Francisque Sarcey has explained how the prayer spoken by *Louis,* ending with

"Que votre volonte soit faite—
    Dieu clement—et la mienne aussi,"

might be spoken in several different ways.

arch, and I really felt sorry for him. He was in genuine distress, so I volunteered to help him. He not only assented, but sat docile as a child. Snatching up a towel, I wiped off the layers of grease-paint he had daubed on. Then I proceeded to give him a quick make-up. It was a hurry-up job, but certainly a hundred per cent. better than he could have executed in his unstrung condition. By degrees his extreme nervousness seemed to subside a bit. Wishing him well, I went around to the front of the house to see the performance. It was weird beyond words. At first the audience sat in dumb amazement; then came titters and giggles, and finally roars. Never did monarch receive less grave and reverent treatment. Boucicault's brogue came out thick and strong. If he had been impersonating *Brian Boru* instead of *Louis XI,* he would have been funny enough, but a French king with a Dublin brogue was too excruciating an anachronism for the audience. To make matters worse, three of the principal parts were also played by Irishmen—John Brougham, Dominick Murray and W. B. ('Billy') Cahill. They all spoke Casimir Delavigne's blank verse 'wid that lovely accint' that one hears on the banks of the Liffey, but never by any chance in Plessis-les-Tours. As the tragedy—or, more properly speaking, the tragic farce—progressed, John Brougham, who loved a good joke better than anything else in the world, began to exaggerate the unctuousness of his own fine, natu-

ral brogue. Next John Clayton,[1] an Englishman
and the son-in-law of Boucicault, who was playing
Nemours, felt in duty bound to fall in line with the
others, and he too assumed a broad brogue. The
rest of the company, either out of deviltry or catch-
ing the infection, became Gaelic instead of Gallic,
and before the play was half over the French tragedy had degenerated into an orgy of Hibernian
dialects. The audience certainly had their money's
worth. Heartier laughter never resounded in a
theatre. People laughed till the tears ran down
their cheeks."

Always intolerant of ridicule, Boucicault did not
enjoy being an object of derision. It is scarcely
necessary to add that his "Louis XI" survived only
a few representations. "Rescued" was again put
on, and it was in this play that John Brougham
made his last stage appearance (October 25, 1879).

Sometime in the eighties, Boucicault was oblig-
ing enough to offer to give a lecture to English
actors then in London, on the correct pronunciation of their mother tongue. The offer was, I
suppose, thought too valuable to be neglected, and
it was arranged that the lecture should be delivered
from the stage of the Lyceum Theatre, Henry
Irving graciously offering the loan of the house
for the occasion.

A report of the proceedings is furnished by Mr.

---

[1] John Clayton (Calthorp) married Eve Boucicault.
Mr. Dion Calthorp, their son, is the author of several
sprightly novels and a most readable book on the evolution of dress in England.

Frank Frankfort Moore in his "Journalist's Note-
Book"; and its humor is not weakened by the frank
admission that it does not give "exact instances"
of Boucicault's Irishisms:

"A more interesting and amusing function I
have never attended. It was clear that the lecturer
had formed some very definite ideas as to the way
the English language should be spoken; and his
attempts to convey those ideas to his audience were
most praiseworthy. His illustrations of the curi-
osities of some methods of pronouncing words
were certainly extremely curious. For instance, he
complained bitterly of the way the majority of
English actors pronounced the word 'war.' 'Ye
prenounce the ward as if it wuz spelt w-a-u-g-h,'
said the lecturer, gravely. 'Ye don't prenounce it
at all as ye shud. The ward rhymes with "par,"
"are," and "kyar," and yet ye will prenounce it as
if it rhymed with "saw" and "paw." Don't ye see
the diffunce?'

" 'We do, we do!' cried the audience; and, thus
encouraged by the ready acquiescence in his pet
theories, the lecturer went on to deal with the gross
absurdity of pronouncing the word 'grass' not to
rhyme with 'lass,' which of course was the correct
way, but almost—not quite—as if it rhymed with
'laws.' 'The ward is "grass," not "graws," ' said
our lecturer. 'It grates on a sinsitive ear like mine
to hear it misprenounced. Then ye will never be
injuced to give the ward "Chrischin" its thrue
value as a ward of three syllables; ye 'll insist on

calling it "Christyen" in place of "Chrischin." D' ye persave the diffunce?'

" 'We do, we do !' cried the audience. 'Ay, and ye talk about "soots" of gyarments, when everybody knows ye shud say "shoots" ; ye must give the full valye to the letther "u"—there 's no double o in a shoot of clothes. Moreover, ye talk of the mimbers of the polis force as "cunstables," but there 's no "u" in the first syllable—it 's an "o," and it shud be prenounced to rhyme with "gone," but not with "gun." Then I 've heard an actor who shud know betther say, in the part of *Hamlet,* "Wurds, wurds, wurds," instead of giving that fine letter "o" its full value. How much finer it sounds to prenounce it as I do, "Wards, wards, wards !" But when I say that I 've heard the ward "pull" prenounced not to rhyme with "dull," as ye 'll all admit it shud be, but actually as if it was within an ace of being spelt "p double-o l," I think ye 'll agree with me that it 's about time that actors learned something of the rudiments of the art of ellycution.'

"I do not pretend that these are the exact instances given by Mr. Boucicault of the appalling incorrectness of English pronunciation, but I know that he began with the word 'war,' and that the impression produced upon my mind by the discourse was precisely as I have recorded it."

Dion also dilated on the fine carriage and grace of the older school of actors, as contrasted with the awkward and slipshod gait of some of the younger generation.

At the conclusion of the lecture, Sir Henry Irving stepped from the lower stage box upon the stage and paid Boucicault a gracious compliment. He said that his early tuition under Boucicault had been of inestimable help to him, and that to Boucicault he owed his first rise from the provinces to London.

CHAPTER XVII

Boucicault barn-storms through America—" The Am-
adan," an imaginative creation—A wonderful repro-
duction of a sea-cave—Irving's desire to play Robert
Emmet, and what frustrated him — He gives the
manuscript to Boucicault—First performance of "The
Jilt" with Dot and Nina Boucicault in the cast—
Boucicault's fount of perpetual youth — He goes to
Australia and marries Miss Thorndyke — Public
indignation at this act—Agnes Robertson's divorce—
Years of futile effort to achieve success — His last
plays and their failure—Starts a school of acting in
New York.

BOUCICAULT never felt himself out-moded.
Younger men with fresher ideas and nervous
enthusiasm pressed forward, but he never said,
"Cedo junioribus." Misfortune dogged him as he
went; one after another, his contributions to the
public maw were spurned; he toured the country[1]
with a company playing these pieces, but the game
was hardly worth the candle, and he returned to
New York as a base of operations.

He found, as time went on, that he had outlived

[1] Mr. Charles Frohman, whose recent death on the *Lusi-*
tania was an incalculable loss to the dramatic universe,
was for a year the treasurer for Boucicault on one of his
road tours. Mr. "Dot" Boucicault, a member of the company, was Mr. Frohman's general stage director in
London.

John Gilbert as *Father Dolan* and Edward Arnott
as *Corry Kinchela* in "The Shaughraun"

This photograph was never issued with the original set owing to the original
negative having been broken

his popularity. He never acknowledged defeat, but he felt the waning respect of the public. As a matter of record, it is necessary to chronicle the last futile works of his pen.

"Vice Versa," anglicized from a Palais Royal farce of the previous season called "Le Truc d'Arthur," was tentatively produced at Springfield, Massachusetts, in 1883, and then brought out at Wallack's. The dialogue was witty and polished, but the situations highly improbable. Boucicault appeared as an ardent Lothario—a very senile lover he was, in faith, who made desperate love to a flirtatious widow, vivaciously acted by Miss Sadie Martinot.[1]

"The Amadan," an Irish play full of sombre effects, received its première at the Boston Museum, Monday, February 5, 1883. It was remotely akin to a French melodrama, "Le Crétin de la Montagne," and the chief character, *Colley,* the "amadan" (usually spelled "omadhan"), was a half-witted boy with a doglike devotion for a beautiful girl who treated him with tender kindness. This part was played in a masterly way by Boucicault. Later, when the piece was produced in New York, his son "Dot," whom he had carefully trained, por-

---

[1] In this play appeared an actor of large physique and expansive personality, Benjamin Maginley by name, a man with a remarkable career. He had been a famous clown in the sawdust ring, and at one time was partner in a circus with James Melville and James Cooke, the foremost equestrians of their day. Even in the ring he had a weighty dignity and belonged to the school of "Shakespearian jesters," à la Wallett, and not to the tumbling

trayed the "amadan," and he himself enacted the
malignant *O'Leary,* a character which, said Mr.
William Winter, "he drew with the revolting col-
ors of absolute truth."

"The Amadan" was one of the most imaginative
of Boucicault's creations, but too sombre to succeed with the general public. One scene, showing
a wild sea-cave, a "puffing-hole," was weird beyond
words, and worthy of Boucicault's best inventive
genius. There are, on the coast of Clare and in
the Arran Islands in the extreme west of Ireland,
natural water-caves with tunnels formed from the
roof upward to the outer surface of the rocks.
These tunnels have been made by the pounding of
the waves alone, when the pressure on the mouth
of the cave was so tremendous that the water had
to seek an outlet elsewhere. It has gradually
bored its way upward clear through the rock.
Consequently, when a storm breaks out, the water
floods the cave and projects powerful streams up
through the roof of the tunnel and out from the
surface of the rock, like a spouting geyser or an
oil-well. In times of storm the waves dash into
the cave and sweep the roof with a thunderous roar
like the boom of artillery.

To try to depict upon the stage a "natural won-

and acrobatic buffoons. With his usual discernment,
Boucicault saw in Maginley the makings of a fine character actor, and engaged him for his company. After two
years with Boucicault, Maginley appeared in David Belas-
co's play "May Blossom," which had a long run at the
Madison Square Theatre. He subsequently starred with
success in "May Blossom."

der" like a "puffing-hole" would have been deemed
impossible by anybody but Dion Boucicault. That
which he undertook to perform he usually accomplished. The scene of the "puffing-hole" in "The
Amadan" was amazing in its illusion; like a Rem-
brandt, it will live in the memory of all who saw
the play. Its attraction for Boucicault seems to
have lain in the fact that it was the most difficult
stage task he could set himself.

Another Irish drama with no less a personage
than Robert Emmet for its hero was acted at Mc-
Vicker's Theatre, Chicago, on Wednesday, November 5, 1884.[1] This play had something of a
history. Early in his career and shortly after his
tenancy of the Lyceum Theatre in London, Henry
Irving was imbued with a desire to portray upon
the stage Ireland's patriot-martyr. The actual
facial resemblance of Irving to Emmet, his physique and bearing, all suggested the Irish patriot;

[1] The cast was as follows:

Michael Dwyer	DION BOUCICAULT.
Robert Emmet	JOSEPH HAWORTH.
Tiney Wolfe	NINA BOUCICAULT.
Andy Devlin	DOT BOUCICAULT.
Lord Kilwarden	J. P. SUTTON.
Lord Norbury	EDWARD CLIFFORD.
Dingley } *Followers of Emmet* {	GUS REYNOLDS.
Finnerty }	WILLIAM STARK.
John Philpot Curran	L. P. HICKS.
Major Sirr	JOSEPH A. WILKES.
Captain Claverhouse . . .	DONALD ROBERTSON.
Father Donnelly	JOHN PAGE.
Sarah Curran	HELEN LEIGH.
Ann Devlin	MARY E. BARKER.
Lady Katherine York . . .	GERTRUDE BLANCHARD.

while the tragic story of Emmet, his romantic love for Sarah Curran, his union with Michael Dwyer, that epic figure in Irish history, seemed rare material for a fine and strong play. Frank Marshall was commissioned to undertake the work, and was rewarded by payments amounting to some six hundred pounds. But just as Irving, after announcing his intention to present the play, was consummating the details of the production, he received a gentle reminder from the British Government that Robert Emmet would be *persona non grata* just then in London. The troubled period of the Land League and agrarian violence had set in, Ireland was in a political turmoil, and an Irish play with so patriotic a figure as Emmet for its hero, and so potential an actor as Irving to incarnate Emmet, might cause untold "ructions." Moreover, Irving ran the risk of being credited with something more than a purely dramatic interest in such a character. So, in deference to the wish of the Government, the project was abandoned.[1]

Frank Marshall's uncompleted manuscript remained on the shelf till, one day, the idea came to Irving that perhaps his old friend and manager might make some use of it. He turned it over to Boucicault, who rewrote it, reshaped it, "boucicaulted" it, and produced it in Chicago. A more inopportune time for the trial of any play could not have been chosen. It was the night of Grover Cleveland's first election to the Presidency, and the

[1] *Vide* Bram Stoker's life of Henry Irving.

city was in a state of feverish suspense and excitement. The next President of the United States was a matter of timelier import than the tragedy of Robert Emmet. So the play did not get an attentive hearing, and Boucicault, losing all heart in it as a "drawing card," never revived it.[1]

"The Jilt" was first acted at the California Theatre, San Francisco, on May 25, 1885. Two of the dramatist's children were in the cast, Dot playing *Geoff Tudor* and Nina playing *Phyllis*. Miss Louise Thorndyke appeared as *Kitty Woodstock,* while the ever-youthful Dion, in a curly brown wig parted down the middle, was *Myles O'Hara,* gentleman-jockey. It was a wonderful exhibition of rejuvenescence in the sexagenarian. Commenting on this phenomenon, "Nym Crinkle," a critic of the day, said:

"I have no patience with an actor who permits us to see that he is growing old. Look at Joe Jefferson and Boucicault! Eros, not Jupiter, pursues them. There is an impertinence in the declaration of the player's work that he is tired. Nay, there is an imposition in it, unless he puts it squarely on his poster and invites us to 'come and see how tired I am of doing this sort of thing.' "

[1] Boucicault sought to persuade Charles Coghlan to undertake the rôle of *Emmet,* and succeeded in arousing his sincere interest in the subject. But when Coghlan read the play and found that Boucicault intended to bring the curtain down on *Emmet* standing before a file of soldiers to be shot, instead of mounting the scaffold to be hung, he refused. He deemed this an artistic mistake as well as a perversion of historical fact.

The most palpable hit in "The Jilt" was the old Yorkshire woman, *Mrs. Welter,* inimitably acted by Mrs. Mary E. Barker. Boucicault thought so highly of her performance that he afterward took her to London for the production of the piece there. Although Mrs. Barker was an American, the London critics pronounced her Yorkshire dialect perfect, and Sir Arthur Wing Pinero, who was not then knighted but plain Mr. Pinero, wanted her to originate a character in a comedy he had completed and was about to bring out. But Mrs. Barker was loyal to Boucicault, with whom she had a contract "till death do us part," and she continued a member of his company till he ceased touring altogether.[1]

"The Jilt" was obviously suggested by Hawley Smart's sporting novel, "From Post to Finish"; but the dramatist's work throughout is of far superior quality to the novelist's. The old wit flashed out again in "The Jilt," and though there was a great deal of sporting slang, it kept the interest alert to the curtain fall.

From San Francisco Boucicault took passage for Australia with Miss Thorndyke, and a marriage ceremony was performed between them, Sep-

[1] Mrs. Barker duplicated her hit in "The Jilt" by her fine characterization of Joan Durbeyfield in Mrs. Fiske's production of Hardy's "Tess of the D'Urbervilles." Mrs. Fiske said she would never give the play without Mrs. Barker, and never did. When Mrs. Barker was killed in an automobile collision, October, 1913, the American stage lost an actress who was rare in her line of character work.

tember 9, 1885, at Sydney.   At first the news was
received with incredulity.   Boucicault had been
known as the husband of Agnes Robertson.   They
had acted together in every part of the United
States and Great Britain as Mr. and Mrs. Boucicault.   They had been received in society as man
and wife.

After obtaining actual proof that the ceremony
with Miss Thorndyke had been performed in
Australia, Agnes Robertson brought suits for divorce both in London and New York, in order to
establish her own marriage to Boucicault, vindicate
her reputation and the legitimacy of her children,
and secure a just allowance as alimony for her and
their support.

These suits for divorce he did not defend.   If
Boucicault had ventured to testify in London, it
was said that he would have been confronted with
his own affidavit made in London, when he claimed
certain property as the husband of Agnes Robertson, and also with a presentation copy of "The Colleen Bawn," sent by him to Queen Victoria, with
portraits of himself and wife inscribed in his own
handwriting.   A divorce was granted to Agnes
Robertson by the British court in the summer of
1888, though the formal announcement was not
made till January 15, 1889.   The court also
awarded alimony, etc., but the defendant escaped
service.   After the divorce, however, he went
through a second marriage ceremony with Miss
Thorndyke in New York.

His last plays were failures, but he never seemed

to lose hope. He was working in sand, but he worked on just the same.

"Fin MacCool," at the Hollis Street Theatre, Boston, February 3, 1887, was a revision of "Belle Lamar." Boucicault wrote in a new part for himself—the title character—an Irish emigrant boy who appears first as a fireman on board a Cunard steamer, working his way out to Boston; is then recruited into the Union army; and after peace is restored between the North and the South becomes a groom in the family of his commanding officer.

"Phryne; or, The Romance of a Young Wife" proved a disappointment at the Baldwin Theatre, San Francisco, September 13, 1887.

"Cushla Machree," his last essay in Irish drama, was brought out in Boston at the Hollis Street Theatre, February 20, 1888. This was "Guy Mannering" done over into Irish. *Meg Merrilies* was transformed into *Morna O'Fail* the "spae-wife," *Dominie Sampson* into *Doctor Poldoodie, Dandy Dinmont* into *Andy Dolan,* and so on. The mellow green moon that rose over Scott's beloved Ellangowan was made to shed its light about Colonel Mannering and the romantic Julia, rechristened and transplanted to "Dunluce's Castle" in the County Antrim. The title "Cushla Machree" signifies "pulse of my heart," but there was no pulse of life in the play. It was one long dribble of dulcet brogue. Boucicault's hand must have lost its cunning. The effect was soporific. For the first time in his career as a caterer to the public, he was downright tedious. The only animation dis-

coverable in the play was in the stage hands, who
were kept busy running "flats" across the boards
or lowering "drops," so that between winks and
nods the spectator could get glimpses of a castle
interior, a forest, a garden, a cabin, a jail, without
troubling himself about their relative sequence.
Meg Merrilies, metamorphosed into a lean and
hungry peasant woman whose taste ran to potatoes
instead of prophecy, was shorn of her supernatural
attributes.   The demolition of a dinner would have
been more tragic than her death, upon which the
curtain fell.

Boston took no pleasure in seeing a mutilated
masterpiece.   But Boucicault, with a strange sort
of obstinate faith in the play, took it to McVicker's
Theatre, Chicago, where, after further revision, he
again forced it upon the public.   This implied a
deliberate refusal on his part to accept Boston's
verdict.   Even more emphatic was Chicago's refusal to accept "Guy Mannering" in an Irish garb.

The failure of this unhappy effort left Boucicault practically penniless.   Till then he had faced
fate bravely, with a courage and resourcefulness
that in a man of his years was more than heroic.
After paying off his people and disbanding his
company he found himself financially "broke."   In
this extremity he wrote from McVicker's in
Chicago to Mr. A. M. Palmer, then manager of
Palmer's Theatre and the Madison Square Theatre
in New York.   It was Boucicault who had once
lifted him out of the slough of ill luck with "Led
Astray," and though they had parted company in

no very cordial relations, they had since "buried the hatchet" and agreed to forget and forgive.

Mr. Palmer certainly harbored no feeling of resentment, for he straightway despatched a reply to Boucicault *in extremis,* offering him the directorship of a "school of acting" which he proposed to organize in connection with the stock company at his Madison Square Theatre. "Number two companies" were then coming into existence, and it was the manager's scheme to recruit road companies for the presentation of his New York successes from the most promising "pupils" in the "school." As drowning men grasp at straws, according to the proverb, so did Boucicault gladly accept this offer. With a touch of genuine dignity, he announced in the columns of the press that he had decided to abandon provincial touring in the future, and seriously to devote the latest years of his life to the good cause of the Drama by teaching the young histrionic idea how to shoot. Pathos and irony are strongly blended in the spectacle of this old man, beyond all question one of the great forces of his time in the world of the theatre, returning penniless to New York to become a teacher of ambitious amateurs at fifty dollars a week.

Great epicure and bon-vivant! He had drunk deep of the wine of success, and now only the dregs remained.

Mighty monarch of the show world! To what petty size had this giant shrunk!

He sought neither pity nor commiseration, and to see him there, bowed and broken, but insouciant as of old, pity was swallowed up in admiration. The wonder was that he still had pluck to fight. His friends could only wish that he had governed his life better.

And it was in no complaining spirit that he took up the drudgery of his last ungracious task. He went to the work with a kind of kingly abandon, "like one who condescended."

CHAPTER XVIII

What Boucicault taught his pupils — Banquet in his honor at the Hoffman House — He dies virtually in harness — Funeral services and last resting-place.

"ALWAYS put your foot down as if to say, 'This spot is mine!'" was the advice Boucicault gave to the young men and women who sat under him at the Madison Square Theatre School of Acting. Then the old man would get up from his chair to suit the action to the word, and his presence, neither great nor imposing, would fill the stage as he measured its length. "The rest of the world may be for whom wills, but where I stand is mine."

Then he would sit down again in his chair, and every student knew he had seen a fine sight. One does not go through the world with the declamatory stride of a stage heroine, but Boucicault at least taught his pupils to put their heels down first instead of walking, as it were, from the toes backward.

"I have never aimed at impossibilities," he was wont to say. "I do not seek to establish a dramatic hothouse in our midst. My aim is to develop the natural gift by inspiration, so to speak, and not to instill mechanical ideas of the great art."

Although Boucicault lagged superfluous, he was not suffered to remain "neglected, forgotten, hang-

ing in monumental mockery like a rusty suit of
mail quite out of fashion." On Saturday night,
November 10, 1888, at the Hoffman House, the
"Saturday Night Club" of New York tendered a
banquet to Boucicault as "the foremost representative of the drama of this age." At his right sat
General W. T. Sherman and Colonel Robert Ingersoll; at his left, Governor Roswell P. Flower and
Mr. Andrew Carnegie. The eloquent Ingersoll was
never more inspired than on this occasion.

The guest of the evening responded to the welcome accorded him in a modest and witty way.

"Sometimes," he said, "when I am passing a
play-bill announcing the performance of one of my
old comedies, I congratulate myself, 'Had I died
forty years ago, I should be living now!' Rather
Irish, perhaps, but it enables me to enjoy a little bit
of '*everness*,' as Bishop Wilkins called it.

"Alas, I wish I had possessed and exercised any
of the influences you ascribe to me, and the drama
would not be now where it is. We should have
had Comedy—that lovely sprite,

" 'The jewels in whose crisped hair
Are set, each other's light to share!'

But the theatregoers (we have no *audience*) will
have none of it! Thalia, like Ophelia, has
drowned in a tank."[1]

[1] Apropos of the then prevailing rage for "tank
dramas," in which real water floated trashy plays to success.

Boucicault was intellectually alive up to the last.

"Turn to Dion Boucicault," said "Nym Crinkle," in his feuilleton, "and you find an alert mind, receptive of every wave of thought, watching every movement of human progress, ready on the instant to talk interestingly on the Munich school of impressionists or the Howells school of realists, familiar with the ultramontane idea and conversant with Ibsen and the whole Russian propaganda, well up in the new Socialism and the new ironclads, but reading 'The Tempest' still, with the imaginative glow of a boy, plus the insight of a philosopher."

He staged "Captain Swift" for Mr. Palmer at the Madison Square Theatre. He adapted "Prête Moi Ta Femme" for Roland Reed. He wrote "The Tale of a Coat" for Sol Smith Russell, and the savage condemnation of this play by the New York press is believed to have hastened his end. It was, at any rate, a bitter blow to the sanguine hopes he had built upon the play's success. At the time of his death he had under way a dramatization of Bret Harte's "Luck of Roaring Camp," and had mapped out the scenario of a play for E. H. Sothern.

He died on the afternoon of Thursday, September 18, 1890, in the apartment-house No. 103 West Fifty-fifth Street. A few weeks before he had had an attack of heart failure, followed by a fainting-spell. But he soon rallied. The man's vigor was amazing; there was in his hardy, sanguine temperament no room for gloomy forebodings. He concealed his condition from his friends, and relaxed not at all the industrious habits that he had acquired in youth and carried into age. Four days before his decease, he had read a new play to a manager, so that he died virtually in harness.

A sudden attack of pneumonia prostrated him; weakness of the heart's action militated against his slender chance of recovery; and when the crisis came he succumbed. He died fully conscious and without pain, attended to the last by his young wife, Louise Thorndyke.

The funeral services were held on Monday, September 22, at the Church of the Transfiguration on West Twenty-ninth Street, affectionately termed, by members of the theatrical profession, "The Little Church Around the Corner." The ritual of the Episcopal Church was read by the Rev. Dr. George H. Houghton.

The "New York Herald" of September 23 said: "Boucicault's last drama was played yesterday for the first and last time. It was witnessed, like so many of the dramas that have gone before it, by an overcrowded and sympathetic house. All of the prominent actors in New York were present. In life they had been his interpreters, giving reality to the figments of his magic brain, and it was seemly that they should come to do him reverence."

His body was temporarily placed in a receiving-vault at Woodlawn. He had expressed an aversion to "fashionable" cemeteries and ostentatious tombs, and his wish was to lie in some sequestered spot. Miss Thorndyke selected a plot in Mount Hope Cemetery, near New York, where, on December 19, 1890, in her presence, his remains were interred.

CHAPTER XIX

WHEN Boucicault went, a link snapped with the last half-century.

If he had been able to read, the morning after his death, the cast-iron obituary notices published by the various newspapers throughout the country, almost identical in phraseology, taken obviously from encyclopedias and not born of knowledge of the man, he would have held up his transparently white hands in holy horror and said:

"For Heaven's sake, is this the mental, moral and physical estimate of one of the greatest intellectualities of his time?"

Few men working for the stage have ever possessed so rare an assemblage of gifts and qualifications as did Boucicault. His knowledge of all departments of the theatre and their resources was complete. His aim and goal were always toward practical achievement. As a pioneer reformer he did giant's service in sweeping away the cobwebs

177

of antiquated tradition which gather as thickly in the manager's office as in the *coulisses*. The practical spirit of the man made him a dominant power "in front" of the house and back on the stage.

In his first success, "London Assurance," he introduced the French fashion of one scene to each act, and this scene a "box set." He reduced the length of dramatic entertainments, which had frequently lasted from seven o'clock till past midnight. Managers were in the habit of offering three or four pieces nightly: he gave one important drama. He abolished the practice of admitting the public for half price at nine o'clock. But the most important of all innovations, and one which wholly changed theatrical conditions both in England and America, was effected by him in 1861. Previous to this year, each prominent theatre had its own company; the "stock" system prevailed; and the great stars from London and New York, when they visited a provincial theatre, were supported by the local "stock." Boucicault contended that such stars would not prove magnets if they did not appear in the new plays in which they had been successful in the metropolis. It was the play, he affirmed, and not the star, that drew the money. He pointed out that the author of such a play received as his royalty a mere pittance—sometimes thirty shillings a night—while the star was paid more than thirty times that amount. Taking advantage of the success of "The Colleen Bawn," he engaged a company of actors, among them John Drew (father of the present actor of that name), Mrs. Hudson Kirby, Mr. and Mrs. John Sloan, and others. He offered the *play* as the *star,* with this satellite company, to the provincial managers. They demurred till one of them consented to give the scheme a trial. The result was an unqualified success. For several years he sent out specially organized companies with his plays, thereby deriving immense revenues. Then followed the disintegration of local "stock companies," till at length few theatres maintained resident companies, but depended solely on touring organizations, which system now prevails generally.

Actors nowadays are often heard anathematizing the memory of Boucicault because he is popularly accredited with originating the matinée. A matinée means to an actor an extra afternoon's work. Boucicault was not guilty of the innovation. The matinée originated in Boston, Massachusetts, where a Puritan "blue-law" of the State of Massachusetts forbade a theatrical performance after sunset on Saturday. The "Hub" managers, to get their six performances a week, instituted an afternoon performance on Saturday. Not a great many years have elapsed since that old Puritan law was repealed.

At rehearsals Boucicault was an exacting martinet; his every word of direction was obeyed with childlike docility, alike by tyros and veterans. Among actors he contrived to create a vast number of enemies: some in the natural way, by his talent and success, which were the most unpardon-

able offenses to one large class of his fellow crea-
tures ; and others by divers and sundry peculiarities
of temper and manner inherent in his hot, hasty
Irish nature.

But they one and all acknowledged him to be a
masterful stage manager.   They carried out his
instructions with enthusiasm and admiration—the
admiration which everything intelligent has for the
higher intelligence.[1]   Just two years before his
death, Boucicault staged Haddon Chambers's play,
"Captain Swift," for A. M. Palmer at the Madison
Square Theatre.   There were unutterable lessons
in the mere sight of the veteran, lively as a cricket,
sharp as a needle, directing Maurice Barrymore,
Holland, Mrs. Agnes Booth, and the rest by the
spell of his intellect.   The result of this laborious
drilling was that when the play was produced not
a reproach could be heard as to the manner of the
representation.

As an actor Boucicault's talent was by no means
limited to the interpretation of the Irish characters
with which his name is popularly associated, and
he shone in volatile French parts, such as *Tourbillon* in Tom Taylor's "To Parents and Guardians"; *Havresac,* in his own little drama, "Napoleon's Old Guard," written when he was a school-

---

[1] It was interesting to note, at a rehearsal at Wallack's,
how actors like John Gilbert, Montague and Mme. Ponisi
obeyed implicitly and without a murmur the dogmas of
the dramatist, sometimes given harshly and always im-
periously.   Montague was never allowed a motion of the
hands, of the feet, of the eyebrows, without an order.

boy at Brentford; *Grimaldi,* in "The Life of an Actress"; and *Mantalini,* in "Nicholas Nickleby."

"His *Counsel for the Defense,* in 'The Trial of Effie Deans,' was perfect," said Edward Stirling, "and might have passed muster in a court of law."

"In such Irish parts as *Conn,*" says Mr. Stephen Fiske, "he has not been surpassed in our day, although Tyrone Power and John Drew may have equalled him."

"This development of actor and author is assuredly a blessed thing," said Clement Scott, "for the reason that the majority of our best plays are and have been written by actors is that these actors have studied the stage for which they wrote, appreciating the value of dramatic effect and understanding the dialogue that the theatre requires. Boucicault, Tom Robertson, R. C. Carton and Pinero are cases in point. They were all actors."

Joseph Jefferson said the same thing, drawing his deduction from a personal example afforded by Boucicault himself, and testifying to Boucicault's fertility in the invention of those bits of "business" which are often more telling on the stage than the most brilliant writing.

When Boucicault played his last engagement in Philadelphia, he was acting in his comedy of "The Jilt." Mr. Jefferson saw part of the play from the front. He entered the theatre just as Boucicault, who was playing the hero, the Irish gentleman-jockey, was bargaining with the villain for some letters which *Sir Marcus Wylie* (the villain) was using for blackmail. The hero's hat was lying on the table, against which he was leaning; *Sir Marcus* had his hat on his head.

In the middle of one of his speeches, Boucicault stopped in his lines, glanced at the noble blackleg's hat, and then, significantly putting his own on his head, continued the conversation. This bit of "business" called forth applause from the gallery and appreciative smiles from the lower part of the house.

"That," said Mr. Jefferson, "is where Boucicault has an advantage over most other writers of plays. He is an actor as well as an author. The literary man would never have thought of introducing that business with the hat."

Every actor of to-day carries a neat speech up his sleeve. At the slightest provocation, out bobs the smiling favorite in front of the curtain to express thanks to his "dear friends," the audience. Sometimes the speech is formal, sometimes pleasantly familiar and confidential, sometimes austere, sometimes genial and humorous, but invariably is it "in behalf of myself and my company."

This delightful way of giving the audience a personal and individual glimpse, as it were, of the actor's real self is gratifying to no one more deeply than to the actor himself. With joyful affability does he bound beaming forth to respond to the vociferous calls for "Speech! Speech!" With radiant good nature—but with what modesty!— does he tell his admirers how truly their applause has inspired himself and his company. What matter if the "illusion" is lost when *Baron Chevrial* or *Caleb Plummer* so suddenly steps out of the picture? Perhaps a few spectators—precious few —are disgruntled. They came to see acting, not to listen to speech-making. The majority in the audience are delighted: they are getting more for their money than they had anticipated.

The modern curtain speech had not gained general vogue in Boucicault's day—not even in his later day; but he was one of the first of the "great stars" thus to take his "dear friends," the audience, into his confidence. As a speech-maker in front of the curtain he was inimitable—*he kept up the illusion.* Tears in his eyes, tears in his voice, on the farewell night of a long engagement! How many audiences parted with him on those last nights, assured and convinced in the softest and blandest tones that their kind applause meant more to him than the hand-clapping of any other audience in any other city! How many audiences have thrilled with pleasure and cordial welcome on "first nights," when *Conn the Shaughraun* came back again to the "sturdiest and best friends he ever knew"! Sure, *Conn* could make every audience feel that it was the only audience he ever cared to play to. What spectator, in sooth, could doubt that genial, infectious smile and that voice with the harp in it?

Yes, Boucicault was as consummate an actor before the curtain as he was behind it, and well indeed did he demonstrate this fact on first nights and at farewells. No audience, knowing that to it was confided the tender keeping of Dion's heart, could fail to cry, "Long life to him!"—and to any audience (when he felt so inclined) was that trust confided!

There was a sardonic streak in Boucicault that at times was strongly felt by all who knew him intimately. Joseph Jefferson once asked him how, with his cynicism, he could write such beautiful lines and give expression to so many homely sentiments in his plays. Boucicault took this as a great compliment and laughed heartily.

"It 's the art of the thing, me boy," he answered with a chuckle. "It 's the art!"

And in the Laura Keene days, at a bohemian dinner where Boucicault presided, the conversation drifted to botany and the guests laughingly compared each other to the various flowers. "And what sort of a flower am I?" asked Boucicault. Quick as lightning, Mrs. John Wood replied, "Oh, you, my dear Dion, are the deadly nightshade." A chill fell upon the feast, and an ominous silence was only dispelled when Boucicault ordered more champagne.

On another occasion an actress of his company said jokingly, "When you get to Hades, Dion, five minutes after you 're dead, you and Pluto will be struggling for the center of the stage."

Boucicault did not relish the joke, and soon

found a pretext for dismissing the lady from his
company.

"The influence of the censorship," said Boucicault somewhat derisively, "is like that of a lady at
a dinner-party controlling in a delicate way the
subjects spoken of."

That curiously heterogeneous mass of individ-
uals known as "the public" was a butt of ridicule
to Boucicault. Public interest in things theatrical
is nowadays artfully stimulated by the press-agent.
In Boucicault's time this altruistic functionary was
unknown. Nevertheless, Boucicault must have
foreseen the advent of the press-agent, for he used
to say, with reference to the intelligence of the
public: "You must first tell them that you are
going to do it, you must then tell them that you are
doing it, and then that you have done it, and *perhaps* then they will understand you."

Boucicault was once asked if he knew any cure
for stage fright. "The only cure for nervousness,
or stage fright," said the veteran, "is to attend to
your business, to concentrate yourself on your
work. Play to the actor, not to the audience."

In 1888, when mutilated versions of Shakespeare were being served in spectacular form at
two New York theatres, Boucicault was asked,

"What about Mrs. Langtry and Mrs. Brown Potter as Shakespearian heroines?"

"If Venus condescended to appear as *Rosalind*," was his reply, "and Hebe consented to perform *Juliet,* Shakespeare's spirit would be there to see and take delight in their efforts. The boys who originally played *Cleopatra* and *Lady Macbeth* doubtless squeaked through those parts in a grotesque manner."

"But did you find these ladies equal to the tasks they undertook?"

"I could not see for looking," answered Boucicault, airily. " 'Mine eyes were made the fools of my other senses.' And were worth all the rest."

Boucicault was the first to suggest the fireproofing of theatrical scenery, and he gave a public demonstration of how easily and cheaply scenery can be made fireproof. Just after the Brooklyn Theatre fire (December, 1876), when nearly three hundred human beings lost their lives, the theatres suffered in attendance for some weeks. Many reforms were inaugurated, but no law was passed concerning fireproof scenery. Boucicault, like all others interested in the restoration of confidence, proceeded to make public demonstration of the fireproofing of scenery.

In the "New York Herald" of December 21, 1876, appeared the following:

"Between one and two o'clock yesterday afternoon, at Wallack's Theatre, Mr. Boucicault, with a few explanatory remarks to quite a large audience interested in the matter, attempted to set fire to a scene saturated with a solution of tungstate of soda and primed with a solution of silicate of soda, suspended over the centre of the stage. A flame equal to the force of one hundred and fifty of the ordinary gas-jets on the stage was directed on the suspended canvas and held there for about two minutes. The canvas did not blaze or smoke. The portions on which the gas flame had been directed broke, fell to the ground, and crumbled into fine ashes on being touched. Several experiments of this kind were made on different parts of the canvas, and always with the same result. A coil of rope was subsequently submitted to the test of fire. The flame seemed to have little or no effect upon it. It did not discolor it to nearly the same extent as the canvas. All the managers present took a deep interest in the operation, and keenly watched every phase of the experiment. Mr. Harry Palmer of Booth's Theatre, as well as Mr. A. M. Palmer of the Union Square, and Mr. McVicker of the Lyceum Theatre, were particularly well satisfied with all they had seen. They intend to apply it immediately, not only on all the new scenery they may be preparing, but on all the scenes at present in use in their respective theatres, as well as on the flies and wings and borders."

Boucicault's timely action had an eminently

soothing effect on the popular nerves. It was taken for granted that so simple a remedy for such an obvious danger would be universally applied. The experiments were commented on all over the United States, and confidence slowly returned. Boucicault himself was inundated with correspondence on the subject, and for the benefit of theatrical managers throughout the country he subsequently wrote to the "Herald," repeating briefly what he knew of the chemical agents that would serve the purpose.

"There are three well-known resisting agents to flame," wrote Boucicault. "They are tungstate of soda, phosphate of ammonia, and sulphate of ammonia. There are two agents used as dressing to the above; these are silicate of soda and chloride of calcium. In naming these materials I use the vulgar names by which they are known. Many persons having patent processes have applied for our assistance in getting their wares into notice. To these there has been only one reply. An effectual process is well known, and the object, being one of public benefit, is opposed to any private enterprise."

If Boucicault's precautionary advice had been followed from that day to this, theatre fires would have been of less frequent occurrence and great properties that have been swept away in an hour would have been saved by that vital dime's worth of prevention which he recommended as a safeguard against the loss of money and the loss of life.

That Boucicault had the love of Ireland deep in his heart's core, none who knew the man could ever doubt. In proof of his sincerity as a patriot I quote from the "Reminiscences" of Mr. Justin M'Carthy:

"Boucicault took great interest in the Irish national movement here and in America, and expressed a frank sympathy with the general action of the Irish parliamentary party. He came to see me several times in the House of Commons during some of our long struggles against this or that ministry; and I had many talks with him in the old conference room on the right of the steps ascending from the cloak-room to the members' entrance into the lobby. I remember having sometimes a sort of wondering doubt as to whether Boucicault could have been forming any idea of offering to help us in our battle by becoming the representative of an Irish constituency. What an auxiliary he would have been, if he could have made up his mind to any such self-sacrificing enterprise! How delightfully he would have chaffed the ministerial orators; with what bewildering dexterity he would have evaded the impending intervention of Mr. Speaker! But Boucicault never made to me any suggestion of the kind, although I feel not the slightest doubt that his declarations of sympathy with the national cause were absolutely sincere; and so we never had the chance of seeing the author and actor of 'Arrah-na-Pogue' in a part entirely new to him, unrehearsed by him, and utterly unexpected by the public."

No stone marks Dion Boucicault's last resting-place, but his Irish plays are his most fitting monument.

"Prolific Boucicault! what verse can scan
   The merits of this many-sided man?
   A stage upholsterer of old renown,
   Is what an enemy would write him down.
   But let the enemy remember still
   How much we owe to Dion's cunning quill.
   What tho' in many of his plays, perchance,
   There may be hints of foraging in France!
   Let us be mindful of the genius shown
   In those as well as others of his own.
   There is a land the playwright has made sweet,
   And found a laurel in the bog and peat.
   Not yet have audiences joy out-worn
   To see the 'Shaughraun' and the 'Colleen Bawn,'
   And *Dazzle* retiréd from the scene,
   While enter *Conn* and *Myles-na-Coppaleen.*"

WILLIAM L. KEESE,

"Actors and Actresses of Great Britain and the United States" (Cassell & Co., New York, 1886).

MISCELLANY

Songs by Boucicault

"THE WEARING OF THE GREEN."

The old street ballad of 1798 and Boucicault's version (1865):

1798

I met with Napper Tandy,
    And he took me by the hand,
Saying, How is old Ireland?
    And how does she stand?
She 's the most distressful country
    That ever yet was seen;
They are hanging men and women
    For the wearing of the green!
      O Wearing of the green,
      O Wearing of the green,
    My native land, I cannot stand,
      For wearing of the green.

My father loved you tenderly,
    He lies within your breast;
While I, that would have died for you,
    Must never be so blest;
For laws, their cruel laws, have said
    That seas should roll between

Old Ireland and her faithful sons
  Who love to wear the green.
    O Wearing of the green,
    O Wearing of the green,
  My native land, I cannot stand,
    For wearing of the green.

I care not for the Thistle,
  And I care not for the Rose;
When bleak winds round us whistle,
  Neither down nor crimson shows.
But like hope to him that 's friendless,
  When no joy around is seen,
O'er our graves with love that 's endless
  Blooms our own immortal green.
    O Wearing of the green,
    O Wearing of the green,
  My native land, I cannot stand,
    For wearing of the green.

1865

O Paddy dear, and did you hear the news that 's
    going round?
The shamrock is forbid by law to grow on Irish
    ground;
St. Patrick's Day no more we 'll keep, his colours
    can't be seen,
For there 's a bloody law again the wearing of the
    green.

I met with Napper Tandy, and he took me by the
    hand,
And he said, "How 's poor old Ireland, and how
    does she stand?"
She 's the most distressful country that ever yet
    was seen,
They are hanging men and women for the wearing
    of the green.

O if the colour we must wear is England's cruel
    red,
Sure Ireland's sons will ne'er forget the blood that
    they have shed.
You may take the shamrock from your hat and
    cast it on the sod,
But 't will take root and flourish there, though
    under foot 't is trod.
When law can stop the blades of grass from
    growing as they grow,
And when the leaves in summer-time their verdure
    dare not show,
Then I will change the colour that I wear in my
    caubeen,
But till that day, please God, I 'll stick to wearing
    of the green.

But if at last our colour should be torn from
    Ireland's heart,
Her sons with shame and sorrow from the dear
    old isle will part;
I 've heard a whisper of a country that lies beyond
    the sea,

Where rich and poor stand equal in the light of
freedom's day.
O Erin, must we leave you, driven by a tyrant's
hand?
Must we ask a mother's blessing from a strange
and distant land?
Where the cruel cross of England shall nevermore
be seen,
And where, please God, we 'll live and die still
wearing of the green.

PAT MALLOY.

At sixteen years of age I was my mother's fair-
haired boy;
She kept a little huckster shop, her name it was
Malloy.
"I 've fourteen children, Pat," says she, "which
Heav'n to me has sent;
But childer ain't like pigs, you know; they can't
pay the rent."
She gave me ev'ry shilling there was in the till,
And kiss'd me fifty times or more, as if she 'd
never get her fill.
"Oh! Heav'n bless you! Pat," says she, "and
don't forget, my boy,
That Ould Ireland is your country, and your
name is Pat Malloy!"

Oh! England is a purty place: of goold there is
no lack—

I trudged from York to London wid me scythe
    upon me back.
The English girls are beautiful, their loves I
    don't decline;
The eating and the drinking, too, is beautiful
    and fine;
But in a corner of me heart, which nobody can
    see,
Two eyes of Irish blue are always peeping out
    at me!
O, Molly darlin', never fear: I 'm still your own
    dear boy—
Ould Ireland is me country, and me name is Pat
    Malloy!

From Ireland to America, across the seas, I
    roam:
And every shilling that I got, ah! sure I sent it
    home.
Me mother could n't write, but, oh! there came
    from Father Boyce:
"Oh! Heav'n bless you! Pat," says she—I hear
    me mother's voice!
But, now I 'm going home again, as poor as
    I began,
To make a happy girl of Moll, and sure I think
    I can:
Me pockets they are empty, but me heart is fill'd
    with joy;
For Ould Ireland is me country, and me name
    is Pat Malloy.

"LIMERICK IS BEAUTIFUL."

Limerick is beautiful,
　　As everybody knows;
The river Shannon, full of fish,
　　Through that city flows;
But 't is not the river or the fish
　　That weighs upon my mind,
Nor with the town of Limerick
　　I 've any fault to find.
　　　　Ochone, ochone.

The girl I love is beautiful,
　　And soft-eyed as the fawn;
She lives in Garryowen,
　　And is called the Colleen Bawn.
And proudly as that river flows
　　Through that famed city,
As proudly and without a word
　　That colleen goes by me.
　　　　Ochone, ochone.

If I was made the Emperor
　　Of Russia to command,
Or Julius Cæsar, or the
　　Lord Lieutenant of the land,
I 'd give my plate and golden store,
　　I 'd give up my army,
The horse, the foot, the grenadiers
　　And the Royal Artillery.
　　　　Ochone, ochone.

I 'd give the crown from off my head,
   My people on their knees;
I 'd give the fleet of sailing ships
   Upon the briny seas;
A beggar I would go to bed,
   And happy rise at dawn—
If by my side for my sweet bride
   I had found my Colleen Bawn.
         Ochone, ochone.

A PEASANT WOMAN'S SONG.

(1864)

(*"A few days ago I stood on the North Wall and
watched the emigrants embarking for the Far
West, as I have stood on the quays of New York
to see them arrive in America. While chewing
the cud of sweet and bitter fancies over this sad
review, and picturing to myself the fate of each
group as it passed, a chord in the old harp, which
every Irishman wears in his breast, twanged in a
minor key and I heard a young Irish wife in the
backwoods of Ohio singing this strain."—D. B.*)

I 'm very happy where I am,
   Far across the say—
I 'm very happy where I am
   In North Amerikay.

It 's lonely in the night when Pat
   Is sleeping by my side,

I lie awake, and no one knows
    The big tears that I 've cried.

For a little voice still calls me back
    To my far, far counthrie,
And nobody can hear it spake—
    Oh! nobody but me.

There is a little spot of ground
    Behind the chapel wall;
It 's nothing but a tiny mound
    Without a stone at all;

It rises like my heart just now,
    It makes a dawny hill;
It 's from below the voice comes out.
    I cannot kape it still.

Oh! little Voice, you call me back
    To my far, far counthrie,
And nobody can hear it spake—
    Oh! nobody but me.

SENTRY'S SONG IN "BELLE LAMAR."

(1874)

Oh! Why did I lave the County Clare
    To sail across the sea?
Oh! Why did I lave you, Mary Meagher,
    Alone to pine for me,
        In far Kilkee?

Agnes Robertson (Mrs. Dion Boucicault) in the title character
in "Jessie Brown; or, The Relief of Lucknow"

The sky is blue, the land is fair,
    And goold, they say, is plenty here;
But oh! the blue of Mary's eye
    Is bluer than your Southern sky,
And the goold I love is the goolden hair
    Of the fairest girl in the County Clare.

"THE O'NEIL."

(1888)

(The proud race of the O'Neils—one of the oldest in Ulster—would accept no honors from the English Court but, like Grania Uiale, stood fiercely at bay.)

A crowned king I cannot be,
No title less contenteth me;
I 'll keep the crown I won by steel,
For I am Owen Roe O'Neil.
To my own blood I will be true,
To my own land allegiance yield;
Ay! by the faith of Owen Roe!
Ay! by the trusty sword I wield!
I bend my head to God alone,
And humble homage to His throne
        I bear alway.
And when O'Neil defends his right,
That He 'll stand near and see the fight
        Is fair—I pray.

CUSHLA-MACHREE.

(1888)

My home by the bog was a cabin so poor,
Till I mended the thatch and I hung a fine dure;
But I worked like a thrush in a hawthorn-tree,
Till I made a sweet nest for my Cushla-Machree.
There is only just room for my love and for me.
So it houlds all I want in this world, d' ye see?
        I would not this minute
        Give something that 's in it
For all the king's riches on land or on sea!

Mr. W. J. Lawrence has kindly furnished me with this record of

Appearances of the
Boucicaults in Dublin

1861—April 1.   Theatre Royal, Dublin.   Mr. and Mrs. Boucicault opened in "The Colleen Bawn" for twenty-four nights.   This was Dion's first appearance in his native city.

1864—Two visits to the Theatre Royal.   (1) Beginning March 28 in "The Colleen Bawn."

(2) Nov. 7, première of "Arrah-na-Pogue."
On Nov. 10, three theatres announced Bou-
cicault plays: "Arrah-na-Pogue" at the
Royal; "The Colleen Bawn" at both the
Queen's and the Prince of Wales's.

1868—Nov. 2–28. Mr. and Mrs. Boucicault at the
Theatre Royal in the second version of
"Arrah-na-Pogue." It was announced at
the time that they were about to retire from
the stage.

1872—Theatre Royal, April 1. Mr. and Mrs.
Boucicault, Sheil Barry and F. Glover in
"The Streets of Dublin"; Dion as *Badger*.
Special local scenery. "Arrah-na-Pogue"
revived on the 15th.

1874—April 20. Mrs. Boucicault (*solus*) in "The
Colleen Bawn," Theatre Royal.

1878—Oct. 28. Theatre Royal. Mrs. Boucicault,
Edmund Falconer and Leonard Boyne in
Falconer's play, "The O'Donoghue's Warn-
ing; or, The Banshee."

1881—Dion's last visit. Opened at the Gaiety
Theatre, Nov. 28, as *Conn,* accompanied
by Sheil Barry and Marie de Grey. Was
prohibited at this time from singing "The
Wearing of the Green" in the character.

Quotable Extracts

No dramatist was happier in writing dialogue than Boucicault. All through his works—even in his most hastily written pot-boilers—are to be found quotable passages admirable not only in advancing the story of the play but delightful in themselves. "He knows more about the grammar of the stage," said Charles Reade, "than all the rest of them put together." And Sir Arthur Quiller-Couch has said, "I cannot recall one of his plays from which I could not make pleasing extracts."

The Irish dramas especially are sprinkled with drolleries of expression, racy of the soil, and with delicate, fragrant passages which captivate by their wit or are irresistible for their pathos.

Where can be found truer Irish humor than in "The Colleen Bawn"? Who but Boucicault could have given us the answer made by *Myles* when asked by *Eily O'Connor* if he still loved her:

"Did n't I leave the world to follow ye? And since then there 's been neither night nor day in my life. I lay down on Glenna Point above, where I see this cottage, and I live on the sight of it. Oh, Eily, if tears were poison to the grass, there would n't be a green blade on Glenna Hill this day."

Again in the same play, the whimsical philosophy with which *Myles* joins the hand of the col-

leen he worships with that of his favored rival:
"When you cease to love her may dying become
you, and when you do die leave your money to the
poor and your widdy to me, and we 'll both forgive
you."

Here are other nuggets from this same rich
mine:

HARDRESS CREGAN. I would not wed my cousin if
she did not love me—not if she carried the
whole County Kerry in her pocket and the
barony of Kenmare in the crown of her hat!

MRS. CREGAN. I hate this man. He was my husband's agent, or what the people here call a
middleman—vulgarly polite and impudently
obsequious.

HARDRESS. Genus squireen—a half sir and a
whole scoundrel.

ANNE CHUTE. I know—a potato on a silver plate.
I 'll leave you to peel him.

DANNY MANN. Beautiful, is it? Och, wurra,
wurra deelish! The looking-glass was never
made that could do her justice; and if St. Patrick wanted a wife where would he find an
angel that 'ud compare with the Colleen Bawn?
As I row her on the lake the little fishes come up
to look at her; and the wind from Heaven lifts
up her hair to see what the divil brings her down
here at all, at all.

CORRIGAN. You may as well answer me kindly
—civility costs nothing.

MYLES. Ow, now, don't it? Civility to a lawyer
manes six-and-eightpence about.

CORRIGAN. What 's that on your shoulder?

MYLES. What 's that to you?

CORRIGAN. I 'm a magistrate and can oblige you
to answer.

MYLES. Well it 's a boulster belongin' to my
mother's feather bed.

CORRIGAN. Stuff'd with whisky.

MYLES. Bedad! How would I know what it 's
stuff'd wid? I 'm not an upholsterer!

FATHER TOM. (*Sings.*) "Tobacco is an Injun
weed." And every weed wants a wathering to
make it come up; but tobacco being an Injun
weed that is accustomed to a hot climate, wather
is intirely too cold for its warrum nature—it 's
whisky and wather it wants. See now, my children, there 's a moral in everything—e'en in a
jug of punch. There 's the sperrit, which is the
sowl and strength of the man. That 's the
whisky. Then there 's the sugar, which is the
smile of woman; without that life is without
taste or sweetness. Then there 's the lemon,
which is love; a squeeze now and again does a
boy no harm; but not too much. And the hot
wather—which is adversity—as little as possible
if ye plaze—that makes the good things better
still.

ANNE CHUTE. Married! The wretch is married, and with that crime already on his conscience he was ready for another and a similar piece of villainy. It's the Navy that does it. It's my belief those sailors have a wife in every place they stop at.

ANNE. And how am I to get home?
MYLES. If I had four legs I would n't ax better than to carry ye, and a proud baste I 'd be.

FATHER TOM. Let us go inside, Myles, I 've a word to say t' ye.
MYLES. I 've lost the key.
FATHER TOM. Sure it 's stickin' inside.
MYLES. I always lock the dure inside and lave it there when I go out for fear of losin' it.

MYLES. Don't be uneasy! It 's only the boys outside that 's caught ould Corrigan thryin' to get off, and they 've got him in the horse-pond.
KYRLE DALY. They 'll drown him.
MYLES. Niver fear, he was n't born to be drowned —he won't sink—he 'll rise out of the world and divil a fut nearer Heaven he 'll get than the top o' the gallows.

In "Old Heads and Young Hearts" there are many piquant passages. Take these for example:

LITTLETON COKE. Character is indispensable to servant maids, but virtue as a word is obsolete;

we have, indeed, a French word like it, *vertu,*
yes—ladies of *vertu* might signify articles of
rarity.　Gold again is the Midian bath of youth,
possessing also a magnetic attraction for every
cardinal virtue, while all the plagues of Egypt
are shut up in one English word, and that is
poverty, the exhibition of which, like that of the
Gorgon's head, turns the hearts of your dearest
friends to stone.

LADY ALICE.　Where 's Kate?

COLONEL ROCKET.　I picqueted her in the hall with
the baggage—brought her up as a soldier's wife
—perfectin' her facings as a light company and
can manœuvre a battalion with any adjutant in
the service.　Look at her walk, thirty inches
regulation pace, head up, left foot forward—
perfection!　That 's the way to put a girl into
the hands of a husband, sir!

LITTLETON.　Ah, beware, Lady Alice, the friend
of a young and lovely woman should have sixty
years at least and hold orders for his qualifica-
tion.

LADY ALICE.　Young man, take my advice.　A
woman never likes her lover to be more careful
of her character than she is herself, or too provi-
dent in his heart's economy.

ROCKET.　My opinion is that a submarine battery
is attached to the keel of the vessel and exploded
by concussion.

LORD POMPION. Bless me! had Guy Fawkes lived in these times what would become of the House of Peers?

JESSE RURAL. May I entreat your sympathy in favor of a subscription I am raising for a poor creature, a widow with eight children.

LADY POMPION. Widows never appear to have less.

ROEBUCK. But is it practicable? Will he?

LITTLETON. Anything is practicable to a lawyer for five hundred pounds.

LADY ALICE. And your—your—ha, ha!—your protestations to me?

LITTLETON. Egad, that's true! I forgot—oh, don't mistake me,—when I offer Miss Rocket my hand, allow me at the same time to express my wild adoration of your ladyship in the abstract; it's a fearful mania of mine.

LITTLETON. I don't think there was a fool in the house whom she did not flirt with through her opera-glass! Every one noticed it—she swept over the stalls, smiling at every eager eye that was fixed on her—damme, she appears to be intimate with the whole subscription—and then the omnibus boxes—oh, that was awful—why, every man in 'em went round into her box— They went by in twos, relieving each other every five minutes like sentries before Whitehall. She made herself the focus for every lorgnette in the pit.

From "Love in a Maze":

COLONEL BUCKTHORNE. My lord, you are welcome to Buckthorne Chase—my home.

LORD MINEVER. Is that a house? So 't is! I positively took it for a rookery!—no offence to your ancestors—no fault of theirs that they did not live in better days than the good old times.

In "London Assurance" these worldly apothegms:

COOL. A valet is as difficult a post to fill properly as that of a Prime Minister!

SIR HARCOURT COURTLY. Tell me, Cool, at what time was my son in bed last night?

COOL. Half-past nine, Sir Harcourt.

SIR H. Half-past nine! Beautiful! What an original idea! Reposing in cherub slumbers, while all around him teems with drinking and debauchery! Primitive sweetness of nature! no pilot-coated, bear-skinned brawling!

MAX HARKAWAY. I 'm a plain man and always speak my mind. What 's in a face or figure? Does a Grecian nose entail a good temper? Does a waspish waist indicate a good heart? Or do oily, perfumed locks necessarily thatch a well-furnished brain?

SIR HARCOURT. It 's an undeniable fact, plain people always praise the beauties of the mind.

MAX. I thought that the first Lady Courtly had surfeited you with beauty.

SIR H. No, she lived fourteen months with me and then eloped with an intimate friend. Etiquette compelled me to challenge the seducer, so I received satisfaction—and a bullet in my shoulder at the same time. However, I had the consolation of knowing that he was the handsomest man of the age. She did not insult me by running away with a damned ill-looking scoundrel.

MAX. That, certainly, was flattering.

SIR H. It was. Max, my honor would have died without it; for in that year the wrong horse won the Derby—by some mistake. It was one of the luckiest chances—a thing that does not happen twice in a man's life—the opportunity of getting rid of his wife and his debts at the same time.

SIR HARCOURT. You will excuse me while I indulge in the process of dressing. That is a ceremony with me superseding all others; and the least compliment a mortal can pay to Nature, when she honors him by bestowing extra care in the manufacture of his person, is to display her taste to the best possible advantage; and so, *au revoir*.

DAZZLE. When the world puts on its nightcap and extinguishes the sun—then comes the bottle! Oh mighty wine! don't ask me to apostrophize. Wine and love are the only two indescribable things in nature; but I prefer the wine because its consequences are not entailed and are more easily got rid of.

MAX. How so?

DAZZLE. Love ends in matrimony, wine in soda-water.

MAX. Do you know him?

DAZZLE. Oh, intimately. Distantly related to his family; same arms on our escutcheon—empty purse falling through a hole in a pocket; motto, "Requiescat in pace"—which means, "Let virtue be its own reward."

MAX. One point I wish to have settled. Who is Mr. Dazzle?

SIR H. A relative of the Spankers, he told me.

MAX. Oh, no, a near connection of yours.

SIR H. Never saw him before I came down here in all my life. Charles, who is Mr. Dazzle?

YOUNG COURTLY. Dazzle, Dazzle, will you excuse an impertinent question?—but who the deuce are you?

DAZZLE. Certainly. I have not the remotest idea.

ALL. How, sir!

Dazzle.   Simple question as you may think it, it
   would puzzle half the world to answer.   One
   thing I can vouch—Nature made me a gentleman—that is, I live on the best that can be procured for credit.   I never spend my own money
   when I can oblige a friend.   I 'm always thick
   on the winning horse.   I 'm an epidemic on the
   trade of tailor.   For further particulars inquire
   of any sitting magistrate.

*"Formosa" contains a good deal of dross and some
   gold.   Bob Saunders, a Cockney dog thief, meeting Sam Boker, ex-pugilist:*

Bob.   Blest if it ain't Sam Boker, the Lightning
   Arm Hitter, the unbought and undefeated!
   Don't yer recollect me?
Boker.   It 's Bob Saunders!   Why, I thought you
   was doing a government job fifteen years ago
   that would last you for the remainder of your
   nateral existence.   How did you ever come back
   from Australia?
Bob.   I got my papers.   The country don't suit me.
   It 's too 'ot.   It 's only fit for a workin' man!
   London is the place for h'interleck!   There 's
   allus some little game a-goin' there.   (*Winks.*)
Boker.   What are you doing?
Bob.   Oh, something or other most of the time.
   I 'm fond of a h'active life, yer see.
Boker.   And so at last ye 've come down to the
   dogs!

Bob. Vell, yer see, I allays vas wery fond of dogs, and then they is a h'interoduction to the best society. If you are caught on the premises you can allays say: "Does yer want to buy a leetle dorg?"

From "The Poor of New York":

Livingstone. The poor! Whom do you call the poor? Do you know them? Do you see them? They are more frequently found under a black coat than under a red shirt. The poor man is the clerk with a family forced to maintain a decent suit of clothes paid for out of the hunger of his children; the poor man is the artist who is obliged to pledge the tools of his trade to buy medicine for his sick wife; the lawyer who, craving for employment, buttons up his thin paletot to hide his shirtless breast—these are the most miserable of the poor of New York.

Tom Badger. Jerusha, ain't it cold! I could play the banjo on my stomach, while all my shivering anatomy would supply the bones.

Old Pete, in "The Octoroon," exhorting the slaves of Terrebonne to look their best at the auction sale of the plantation:

Cum yer now—stand round, 'cause I 'se got to talk to you darkies—keep dem children quiet— don't make no noise, de missus up dar hear us.
Solon. Go on, Pete.

PETE.   Genl'men, my colored friends and ladies, dar 's mighty bad news gone round. Dis yer prop'ty to be sold—old Terrebonne whar we all ben raised is gwine—dey 's gwine to tak' it away—can't stop here nohow.

ALL.   Oo!—oo!

PETE.   Hold quiet, you trash o' niggers! T'ink anybody wants you to cry? Who 's you to set up screechin'? Be quiet! Cum, for de pride of de family, let every darkey look his best for de Judge's sake—dat ole man so good to us, and dat ole woman—so dem strangers from New Orleans shall say, dem 's happy darkies, dem 's a fine set of niggers; every one o' you say when he 's sold: "Lor' bless dis yer family I 'se gwine out of and send me as good a home."

In "The Shaughraun" Boucicault is probably at his best, as the following extracts abundantly prove:

CLAIRE FFOLLIOTT.   (*At the churn.*)   Go on now, Mrs. O'Kelly, and mind your own business. Do you think I 'm not equal to making the butter come?

MRS. O'K.   It 's yourself can make the butter come. You have only got to look at the milk and the butter will rise of itself.

FATHER DOLAN.   Did n't you give me a promise last Easter that you would leave off dhrink?

CONN. I did—barrin' one thimbleful a day just to take the cruelty out of the wather.

FATHER D. One thimbleful. I allowed you that concession. No more.

CONN. God bless ye, ye did. An' I kep' my word.

FATHER D. Kept your word! How dare you say that? Did n't I find you ten days after stretched out as dhrunk as a fiddler at Tim O'Malley's wake?

CONN. Ye did, bad luck to me!

FATHER D. And you took only one thimbleful?

CONN. Divil a dhrop more—see this. I could n't refuse one dhrink out of respect to the corpse— long life to it! But as luck would have it, there was only one thimble in the place, and that was a tailor's thimble, an' they could n't get it full. Egorra, but they got me full first.

At Conn's Wake:

MRS. O'K. You are kindly welcome. The dark cloud is over the house, but—

CLAIRE. Did they bring him home insensible?

MRS. O'K. No, miss, they brought him home on a shutter, an' there he lies now wid his dog Tatthers beside him. The crathur won't let a hand go near the body.

BIDDY (*professional mourner at the wake*). Good luck t' ye, give me a dhrop o' something to put the sperrit in me. None was like him—none could compare, and he was brave! he was open-handed! He had the heart of a lion and the legs of a fox.

> (*Conn takes the jug, empties it quietly, and, unobserved by all, replaces it on stool.*)

BIDDY. His voice was softer than the cuckoo of an evening, and sweeter than the blackbird after a summer shower. Weep, ye colleens, ye 'll never hear the voice of Conn again.

CONN (*sotto voce*). It 's a mighty pleasant thing to die like this, once in a way, and hear all the good things that are said about ye afther you 're dead and gone, when they can do you no good.

BIDDY. His name will be the pride of the O'Kellys forever more.

CONN (*aside*). I was a big blackguard when I was alive.

BIDDY. (*Taking up her jug.*) Oh, he was sweet and sthrong—Who the divil 's been at my jug of punch?

From "Arrah-na-Pogue":

BEAMISH MACCOUL (*the patriot*). See, the morning is beginning to tip the heights of Mullacor; we must part. In a few hours I shall be on the sea, bound for a foreign land; perhaps never again shall I hear your voices or see my native hills. Oh, my own land! my own land! Bless every blade of grass upon your green cheeks! the clouds that hang over ye are the sighs of your exiled children, and your face is always wet with their tears. *Eirne meelish, shlawn loth!* Fare ye well! And you, dear Abbey of St. Kevin, around which the bones of my fore-fathers are laid!

On the way from the chapel, the wedding party stop at the house of Colonel Bagenal O'Grady:

O'GRADY. Thank ye, Shaun, and may this day, that will change the name of your bride, never change the heart of Arrah-na-Pogue.

FANNY POWER. Arrah-na-Pogue! that means Arrah-of-the-Kiss!

O'GRADY. Don't you know why she is called so? Tell her, Arrah!

ARRAH. Sure I do be ashamed, sir.

SHAUN. Ah, what for? It 's proud I am of the kiss you gave, though it was n't meself that got the profit of it.

FANNY. Indeed; and who was the favored one?

SHAUN. Beamish MacCoul, miss; her *comdaltha* —I mane her foster-brother, that is. It was four years ago. He was lyin' in Wicklow Gaol, the day before he was to be hung wid the rest of us, in regard of the risin'.

FANNY. I remember, he escaped from prison the day before his execution.

SHAUN. Thrue for ye, miss. The boys had planned the manes of it, but could n't schame any way to give him the office, because no one was let in to see the masther, barrin' they were searched, and then they could only see his face at a peep-hole in the dure of his cell.

FANNY. Did Arrah succeed in conveying to him the necessary intelligence?

SHAUN. She did. Bein' only a dawny little creature at that time, they did n't suspect the cunnin' that was in her; so she gave him the paper in spite of them, and under the gaoler's nose.

FANNY. How so? You say they searched her. Did they not find it?

SHAUN. No, miss. You see, they did n't search in the right place. She had rowled it up and put it in her mouth; and when she saw her foster-brother, she gave it to him in a kiss.

ARRAH. And that 's why they call me Arrah-na-Pogue.

FANNY. No one but a woman would have thought of such a post-office!

And, to conclude, let me add the droll speech of Myles O'Hara, the gentleman jockey, in "The Jilt":

As my poor father lay on his death-bed he held me by the hand. He squeezed it softly. I knew he was going. "Myles," he said, "my darling boy, stoop down." And he whispered, "Never put your money on a mare," and he died.

Chronological List of Boucicault's Dramatic Works

SHAKESPEARE IN LOVE................London, 1846
LOVE AND MONEY....................London, 1847
THE WILLOW COPSE ....London, 1848
THE KNIGHT OF ARVA...............London, 1848
SALAMANDRINE ....London, 1849
GIRALDA ....London, 1850
THE INVISIBLE HUSBAND.............London, 1850
A RADICAL CURE....................London, 1850
THE BROKEN VOW....................London, 1851
L'ABBAYE DE CASTRO................London, 1851
LOVE IN A MAZE....................London, 1851
SEXTUS THE FIFTH..................London, 1851
THE GARDE MOBILE..................London, 1851
THE QUEEN OF SPADES...............London, 1851
PAULINE ....London, 1851
THE CORSICAN BROTHERS.............London, 1852
THE VAMPIRE.......................London, 1852
THE PRIMA DONNA...................London, 1852
GENEVIEVE ....London, 1853
THE YOUNG ACTRESS...............New York, 1853
THE FOX HUNT; OR, DON QUIXOTE II.New York, 1853
ANDY BLAKE ....Boston, 1854
FAUST AND MARGARET................London, 1854
LOUIS XI..........................London, 1854
PIERRE THE FOUNDLING..............London, 1854
EUGENIE ....London, 1855
JANET PRIDE ....London, 1855
APOLLO IN NEW YORK..............New York, 1855
THE CHAMELEON ....New Orleans, 1855
THE FAIRY STAR.....................Boston, 1855
THE LIFE OF AN ACTRESS.........New Orleans, 1855
THE PHANTOM...................Philadelphia, 1856
AZAEL ....New Orleans, 1856
UNA ....New Orleans, 1856
NOTHING IN IT.................Philadelphia, 1856

BLUEBELLE ....New York, 1856
THE CAT CHANGED INTO A WOMAN.....Boston, 1856
GEORGE D'ARVILLE...................London, 1857
THE POOR OF NEW YORK............New York, 1857
WANTED—A WIDOW...............New York, 1857
PAUVRETTE (also acted under the titles
  "SNOWFLOWER" and "THE SHEP-
  HERDESS OF THE ALPS")...........New York, 1858
JESSIE BROWN; OR, THE RELIEF OF
  LUCKNOW ....New York, 1858
DOT (THE CRICKET ON THE HEARTH).New York, 1859
CHAMOONI THE THIRD..............New York, 1859
SMIKE (NICHOLAS NICKLEBY) ......New York, 1859
THE OCTOROON; OR, LIFE IN
  LOUISIANA ....New York, 1859
THE TRIAL OF EFFIE DEANS (HEART
  OF MIDLOTHIAN) ....New York, 1860
VANITY FAIR; OR, PROUD OF THEIR
  VICES ....New York, 1860
THE COLLEEN BAWN; OR, THE BRIDES
  OF GARRYOWEN..................New York, 1860
LADY-BIRD; OR, HARLEQUIN LORD
  DUNDREARY, a pantomime..........London, 1862
ARRAH-NA-POGUE; OR, THE WICKLOW
  WEDDING ....Dublin, 1864
RIP VAN WINKLE; OR, THE SLEEP OF
  TWENTY YEARS...................London, 1865
HOW SHE LOVES HIM.............New York, 1865
THE PARISH CLERK..............Manchester, 1866
THE LONG STRIKE...................London, 1866
THE FLYING SCUD; OR, A FOUR-LEGGED
  FORTUNE ....London, 1866
HUNTED DOWN; OR, THE TWO LIVES OF
  MARY LEIGH......................London, 1866
A WILD GOOSE CHASE...............London, 1867

AFTER DARK ....London, 1868
FOUL PLAY (written with Charles
    Reade) ....London, 1868
DREAMS (written with T. W.
    Robertson) ....New York, 1869
PRESUMPTIVE EVIDENCE ....London, 1869
FORMOSA; OR, THE RAILROAD TO RUIN...London, 1869
PAUL LAFARGE; OR, SELF-MADE.......London, 1870
A DARK NIGHT'S WORK..............London, 1870
LOST AT SEA (written with Henry J.
    Byron) ....London, 1870
THE RAPPAREE; OR, THE TREATY OF
    LIMERICK ....London, 1870
JÉZEBEL; OR, THE DEAD RECKONING....London, 1870
ELFIE; OR, THE CHERRY TREE INN......London, 1871
KERRY; OR, NIGHT AND MORNING.......London, 1871
BABIL AND BIJOU....................London, 1872
JOHN BULL (altered from Colman).....London, 1872
A MAN OF HONOR.................New York, 1873
LED ASTRAY ....New York, 1873
MORA; OR, THE GOLDEN FETTERS.....New York, 1873
DADDY O'DOWD (also acted under the
    titles, "THE O'DOWD" and "SUIL-A-
    MOR") ....New York, 1873
MIMI ....New York, 1873
MERCY DODD ....Philadelphia, 1874
BELLE LAMAR ....New York, 1874
THE SHAUGHRAUN.................New York, 1874
FORBIDDEN FRUIT ....New York, 1876
THE BRIDAL TOUR ....New York, 1877
CLARISSA HARLOWE................New York, 1878
MARRIAGE ....New York, 1878
CONTEMPT OF COURT..............New York, 1879
RESCUED ....New York, 1879
SPELL-BOUND ....New York, 1879

Vice Versa................Springfield, Mass., 1883
The Amadan........................Boston, 1883
Robert Emmet.....................Chicago, 1884
The Jilt.......................San Francisco, 1885
Phryne; or, The Romance of a
    Young Wife.................San Francisco, 1887
Fin MacCool.......................Boston, 1887
Cushla-Machree ....Boston, 1888
The Tale of a Coat...............New York, 1890
Lend Me Your Wife.................Boston, 1890
The Luck of Roaring Camp.......New York, 1892

(There are still extant, also, a few copies of "A Child's History of Ireland," privately printed in Dublin, and afterward reprinted by James Osgood, Boston, Mass., 1880, under the title, "The Story of Ireland.")

Townsend Walsh.